PROMISES TO KEEP

'A Collection of Short Stories'

Tom McDonald

Bluewater Publication
Killen, AL 35645
Bluewaterpublications.com

Published in the United States by Bluewater Publications.
Printed in the United States of America.

This work is based on incidents from the author's personal perspective.

Interior Art by Jackie Hastings
Cover Designed by Scott Campbell
Page Designed by Maria Yasaka
Edited by Sierra Tabor

This book is dedicated to the memory of my oldest brother, Bill, or William Lindsey McDonald, as many knew him.

Table of Contents

Credit

The cabin depicted on the cover is the one mentioned in the title chapter, "Promises to Keep." It was built by my father and our cousin, Frank Rickard, right after the Great Depression. As young boys, some of my older brothers helped with its construction.

Before his death, my oldest brother, Bill, asked me to try and determine if the old cabin was still standing. I suppose in his mind it was a direct link to his boyhood and seemed to be very important to him. During the long search, my cousin Mary Hughes, daughter of Frank Rickard, mentioned that a friend had painted the old cabin from a photograph and given it to her as a gift. The name of her friend on the original painting was Imogene Butler. Mary was gracious enough to take a picture of the painting and send it to me. My cousin Mary passed away a few months after I received the package.

This photograph of the painting provided me and my wife a concrete image of the object of our search. Otherwise, our efforts would most certainly have been in vain. A posthumous thank you is due to my late cousin Mary and her thoughtful friend, Imogene Butler.

A Special Thank You

I would be extremely remiss if I didn't once again thank my good friend Jackie Hastings for the beautiful drawings preceding each chapter of this newest book. This man has more talent than Carter has little liver pills. Maybe some of the older readers will understand this reference. Jackie's drawings have graced each of my books, and I am eternally grateful for his talent and his friendship. However, as much as I admire my friend's talent, it is over-shadowed by his love for our Lord and Savior Jesus Christ and his unfailing willingness to share that love with those around him.

Acknowledgments

It is difficult to believe that my third book has now been published. The task of acknowledging each and every individual who played a role in this miracle is beyond my limited ability.

Certainly, my family has encouraged me and helped me through some rough patches. Without the more than able assistance of my wife, Margo, I would still be writing stories on napkins and envelopes and hiding them in the bottom of my sock drawer. She has been a source of quiet courage and inspiration since we were in high school together.

Even farther back than high school, I want to acknowledge the contribution of a group of stalwart and serious ladies: my elementary school teachers at Brandon School in Florence, Alabama. These ladies were tasked with the unenviable job of educating the sons and daughters of what many today would call the working lower class. We really did literally live on the wrong side of the tracks and we knew it. My roots are there and, sort of like the roots of a maple tree, they surface from time to time and cannot be overlooked. Thank you, Mrs. Sullivan, Mrs. Smyrl, Mrs. Floyd, and Mrs. Dillard, for doing your very best to make a silk purse out of a sow's ear. And, one more thing: thank you, Mrs. Elsie Dillard, for reading Bible stories to your class of knuckle-headed sixth graders. I remember them to this very day.

Introduction

While attending law school at the University of Alabama, the late Harper Lee decided that her true calling in life was writing, not the study of law. Her first novel, *To Kill a Mockingbird*, a story of growing up in a small southern town, was awarded the Pulitzer Prize in literature. She was the first author to have her first and only book receive this coveted award. As with much of life, what we believed to be true turned out to be wrong. Much to the surprise of the experts, Ms. Lee had written an earlier novel which no one knew existed. This book, *Go Set a Watchman*, has now been published.

My books have absolutely nothing in common with the marvelous work of Harper Lee. They should not be mentioned in the same sentence. However, Ms. Lee did hold true to one axiom of writing that I have found to be very valuable. She is quoted as saying that if one is going to write, he "should write about what he knows."

Therefore, following the advice of Harper Lee, I will never write a book about my love for math, how to set a proper table, basking in the main stream of political thought, engaging in small talk with folks who need to get a life, or a whole host of other topics which cause my gout to flare up.

The only reality I know is what has happened to me during the course of my life. Those are the things I write about. Some folks have told me the stories make for good reading. Others have said something quite different.

Average is Normal

In graduate school one of the most difficult courses required for my degree was in statistics. Maybe it was because my brain is somewhat adverse to numbers and gets over-loaded rather quickly. In that class we were taught about the standard error of measurement, the bell-shaped curve, what it takes to constitute a statistical difference between certain known factors, and more than I ever wanted to know about the mean, median, and mode. When it was all over, it seemed the bottom line to the whole course was centered on how to determine what is average and how far different things we think are important deviated from what was considered to be average. Statistics are very important in the field of education, particularly in the area of testing. In addition, they are now playing an increasingly important role in our everyday lives. In some way or another, we are all just a bunch of statistics.

Society seems to be obsessed with what constitutes average in areas of our lives that are personal and should be nobody's business. We know the height, weight, shoe size, intelligence level, salary, church preference, and the number of pickles consumed in a year by the average American male. Baseball enthusiasts can recite the average of every player in areas such as hits, runs, strikeouts, doubles, triples, bases stolen on Tuesdays, number of times hit by a ball thrown by a bald headed pitcher over six feet tall, and the list seems to never end. Life insurance companies employ actuaries who can determine statistically when we will probably die. This allows them to compute an appropriately high premium while we are alive and not lose money on our policy when we kick the bucket. Insurance companies are like casinos: they cannot stay in business if the odds are not in their favor.

Our government is absolutely obsessed with statistics, in some ways for the good and in some ways, not so good. After retiring from my teaching career, I worked for the United States Census Bureau. This agency happens to be the greatest collector of statistics in the history of the world. Enumerators who go door-to-door are required to ask questions which to most folks seem to be a violation of their privacy. As a manager I was often confronted with enraged citizens demanding to know why certain bits of information were necessary. For example, we had to ask citizens how many commodes were in their homes. The question seems intrusive but the reason behind the question makes a little bit of sense. The average number of commodes per household in a given area apparently was important to the federal government in determining which areas of our country needed new and improved water service lines and sewage treatment systems. I must say that this little bit of information generally failed to placate the most highly enraged of our citizenry.

My point is that somewhere, someplace there are statistics kept on everything we can imagine and some things we cannot imagine. We have all heard the adage that "statistics don't lie." This is true, but the other side of that coin is that "liars use statistics." In other words, numbers can be used to prove almost any point if you twist them around enough. Ample evidence is available on a daily basis when we watch various experts on television twist, distort, and misrepresent figures to prove whatever point they are hung-up on at any particular time. It is amazing that two people can use the exact same statistics to prove points which are polar opposite of each other. This fixation on numbers will only get worse as everyone from six years old and up can call up any statistic ever created on their Smart Phone in a matter of seconds. Even someone with a technological deficiency like me can "Google" most anything and come up with numbers and facts which "boggle" my brain. Sometimes I fear we have abandoned a normal existence which could certainly be made much better by technology. Instead, we have allowed technology to become our reason to exist.

It has occurred to me that I am above average in some areas and below average in many others. This is true for all of us. For example, I am above average in weight and the number of Krispy Kreme doughnuts consumed per year. In the statistics course I had to take in college, this would be called a direct correlation between these two factors in that the more doughnuts I eat the heavier I become. It has been my experience that the above average statistics many folks claim as their own have more to do with bragging rights than with their quality of life.

Several years ago my wife and I were doing volunteer work at the building which once housed Brandon School where my whole family attended as children. This lengthy list includes my grandparents, parents, siblings, aunts, uncles, cousins, and quite a few others who had fallen off the family tree. Some enjoyed the experience so much they repeated a few grades just to make sure they didn't miss anything. The building and property had been purchased by the Methodist Church and was being renovated to be used in various church ministries. The many artifacts and records from years past when it was a community school had been stored in one room. The school had been such a big part of my family's past, I asked the custodian if I could browse through the room, and he was kind enough to allow me to do so. As I looked at the class pictures and other items stored in the room, I was flooded by memories from that time in my life. It is amazing what is locked away in our brain just waiting for something to trigger a tidal wave of memories. Perusing the record file, I found my information card from the sixth grade. On this card was recorded information about the McDonald family, including results from intelligence tests schools have been so fond of administering. I found the I. Q., or intelligence test scores, of my siblings and even some of my cousins on adjacent cards. It occurred to me that this information was really none of my business but did involve me personally. Besides, how would they ever know if I didn't tell them? Quite contrary to what the government might believe, I believe that any information about me is my business. At this point, my ego took over because at my fingertips was information that would prove I was smarter than any of my older brothers had ever admitted. Much to my dismay, my score was the lowest of the entire family. According to what I learned in my statistics course in college, my score was "several points below the mean but less than one standard deviation from the norm."

After recovering from the shock, I became even more convinced that there is a real danger in using test scores to categorize students. Using just the test scores from that one card, many professional educators would conclude that my potential as a student was very limited. Basically, it could be interpreted that any schooling beyond grade school would be a challenge. In fact, in some countries this would have been enforced by government policies, and I would have been denied the opportunity to continue my education. Higher education would never have been a reality for me. One real nugget I took from my statistics class was that tests never measure anything perfectly, and we should all keep that in mind when we have a tendency to define people with a number. We are more than a number and should never use only numbers to place limits on anyone's potential.

Our society today tries to pretend none of our children are merely average. They are recognized as superior for every endeavor they have ever attempted. This policy may prove to be a big mistake when the real world comes a-knocking. Our children's rooms are embellished by more trophies, plaques, certificates, and sundry awards than the walls of many politicians' offices. Every election year these same politicians proclaim they want schools which guarantee every student will score above average on achievement tests. Another thing I learned in statistics is that it is impossible for everyone to be above average in anything. The only way for the above average elite to attain that label is because there's always an equal number of us common rabble in the below average category. Whether this is good or bad is a debate best left to their parents, polo coaches and child psychologists. I no longer have a dog in that fight. However, for many years I did have a dog in that fight and my dog often lost. My job as a school counselor included some responsibilities to the school system as a psychometrist. This meant I was called upon to administer tests, individual and group, to students for various purposes. Much to my dismay, I found that many parents are infatuated with the I. Q. score of their child. It sort of defines their child in the parent's eyes. Many are guilty of using this number to determine what their child might be capable of accomplishing. The stress many parents inflict on their child who might have a high intelligence test score can seriously affect the relationship between parent and child. Thank goodness, my parents had no clue about test scores, especially low ones. There are times when ignorance is bliss.

But the point of all this is the injustice of it all. Constantly comparing ourselves to others leads to nothing but despair about our own life. Even worse, it causes some of us to look down on others. Differences are used as excuses to exclude others from the very things we often seek to enjoy only for ourselves and those like us. We are categorized as being average by a society which places great emphasis on defining people by factors that frequently have no bearing on the real person who lives inside their skin.

During my very first year as a teacher, I taught science to seventh and eighth graders. All the students had been previously categorized as advanced, average, or below average by written tests and placed in the appropriate level in all their academic classes. Since I was a new teacher, I was assigned to teach all the below average science classes. Low and behold, one of my students actually won the Science Fair that year with his project. Winning the Science Fair was a very big deal at that time. He very clearly demonstrated visually how tornadoes were formed, and it was a wonderful project. The teacher of the advanced science classes sought to have him disqualified because he was in the below average class. Basically, she felt that his success made the school look bad. Unfortunately, this mind-set is shared by more than a few educators to this very day. The point is that by categorizing people we frequently do them an injustice, and that applies to many areas, not just in our schools.

Be that as it may, we are at the mercy of others when it comes to being evaluated and labeled in our daily lives, and most often it is out of our control. But, thank goodness, there is one exception. There is a light at the end of the tunnel, pun intended. We have control of our own destiny when it comes to our spiritual life. It matters not what others think when it comes to our relationship with God. This is something that falls exclusively on our own shoulders. We can be average or below if we choose. The great thing is that we can develop a relationship with God that makes all these other factors insignificant and meaningless. Our Heavenly Father looks inside each of us before passing judgment. The sincerity of this relationship comes strictly from within and cannot be determined by anything external. Class rank and GPA become as worthless as a side saddle on a hog. In First Samuel, the Bible tells the story of God sending the prophet Samuel to anoint David as the next king of Israel. Samuel was not told who this person would be but only that the new king would be one of the sons of a man named Jesse. Samuel's task was to simply go and anoint the one God had already chosen. But none of the big, strong men paraded past him were acceptable. Finally, David, the smallest and youngest of Jesse's sons, and presumably the least acceptable by physical standards, was summoned from the fields where he was tending the sheep. God told Samuel, "This is the one, anoint him." Earlier in this same chapter of the Bible we read that, "The Lord doesn't see things the way you see them. People judge by outward appearance, but the Lord looks at the heart."

Society seems to go overboard in search of incredibly superficial means of categorizing people, but this is not a problem with our Creator. God does not look for perfection and impressive statistics but calls out to those who are not perfect and know it. It is highly likely that some folks are too proud or impressed with themselves to be used in any significant way. On many occasions, the Bible warns us that pride can be our downfall. On the other hand, it is highly likely that if we could be a little less impressed with ourselves and more thoughtful toward others, the world would be a much better place to live.

To be truthful, there are far more anonymous ordinary people on this planet than geniuses. God did not use super heroes to change the world but, instead, used simple, broken, ordinary people who relied on Him for their strength. He has given each of us individual talents and does not rank his children and compare them in terms of worthiness. In other words, God does not use statistics!

******

Bad Trips and Wrong Turns

Eons ago, during a time barely remembered, my life was vastly different. In other words, I was gainfully employed. Regardless of the timeline, my first real job in my chosen profession was to make a valiant effort to teach science to junior high kids. Teaching junior high kids anything is a miracle in itself, but someone has to do it.

Many of us remember from our junior high science class there are basic machines from which all inventions are derived. Others among us do not remember ever having a science class, or even attending school for that matter. Be that as it may, the facts as we understood them were that simple machines, either by themselves or compounded together, were responsible for all the inventions of mankind. At least that was the story at the time. However, this story may have evolved just as so many other things have over the years. A perfect example would be in the political world of today. Politicians have perfected this policy of "evolved thinking." It now means that perhaps I can get more votes if I think like this instead of the way I was thinking before. And tomorrow, being a new day, I may see a totally different point of view.

Apparently science, like my waistline and the thought process of politicians, is constantly changing. The science textbook we used during my first year as a teacher was embarrassingly out of date. One bit of evidence was that it emphatically stated space travel was something most of us would not live to see in our lifetime. The year I stood before my first science class as a teacher was 1968. If I recall correctly, on July 20, 1969 Neil Armstrong was delivered to the moon by Apollo 11, and as he stepped from his flimsy space craft, he said something to the effect, "One small step for man, one giant leap for mankind." It took many years for this "giant leap for mankind" to reach the classroom. Unfortunately, for many, it has not yet arrived.

The book was also of the opinion there were nine planets revolving around the sun: our planet Earth was one of the nine. For some reason, I spent a lot of time on the rather obscure planet named Pluto possibly because of the Disney character with the same name. An apology to my former students may be in order at this point, because science has now concluded that Pluto may not actually be a real, bona fide planet. Today's experts seem to agree that what they believed to be a real planet is only a mass of hot gasses. Some of my students had the same opinion of me. I am so sorry about that, especially if one incorrect answer regarding Pluto on a final exam resulted in a failing grade for the course. You see, in those days, teachers felt keeping a few "retreads" around for a second year of the same class might serve as motivation for the new arrivals. Apparently, that line of thinking has also evolved and new policies are in place. The new policy seems to center around the fact that we must never hurt anyone's feelings by simply assigning them the failing grade they managed to earn all by themselves. Those who are in charge of our schools have decided that the self-concept of a student is very fragile and must be massaged constantly. Before we move on, I have one final message for my former students: remember, I told you many times that one of the absolute facts that will never change is that life is not fair.

Other than some apparent misinformation regarding the planetary system, I also spent a lot of time trying to teach junior high students about simple machines and how they have changed our society. Some common examples of basic machines include such things as the wedge, the lever and the wheel and axle.

Theoretically, without these simple machines, we would not have the luxury of modern day heating and cooling systems. Nor would we have computers or cell phones or flushing toilets. We would be without the light bulb, the ball point pen, or that marvelous invention which reminds us what we are to do tomorrow, the refrigerator magnet. Lastly, where would the world be today without the wheel and axle which brought us the automobile? Those who find this theory hard to believe have the same mindset as my former students.

Over the last century or so, the automobile has pretty well defined America. Our nation has become known world-wide for our dependence on the automobile as a primary means of transportation. Some folks in other countries utilize mass transportation such as the train to move from place to place. Others still use the bicycle for personal conveyances over relatively short distances. A word of caution: history has shown that nations which depend upon the bicycle as a major means of transportation will eventually witness German troops goose-stepping down the main thoroughfare of their capital city. That fad will never catch on in this country, because it would be a personal affront to most Americans to stoop to the level of riding a bicycle except to show off sporty new exercise clothing. Besides, it is virtually impossible to text while riding a bike.

These machines are undeniably useful and have their place in certain areas of the world but, apparently, not in the United States of America. Practically every red-blooded American comes into this world dreaming of the day they will own their first car. We can't wait until the time arrives when we can climb behind the wheel and experience a level of independence and freedom only the open road and an incredibly fast car can provide. Another word of caution: those in the market for a very fast car should be skeptical of the four-cylinder models which sport a speedometer which indicates the vehicle is capable of reaching a speed of 140mph. The scientific term for this blatant lie is called an optical illusion or a clever marketing strategy.

This wonderful machine we call the automobile is capable of delivering its occupants to practically any destination we so desire, or, in some cases, destinations we do not desire to be and are left wondering how in the world we ever got there in the first place. The phenomena of being lost is not a new experience for me. I have often been lost and could not blame it on road maps or sudden wrong turns while behind the wheel. I have been sort of lost at the local mall when I drove Margo's car and then, upon exiting, spent the better part of an hour searching for my truck, which was still parked at home. On one occasion, after breathlessly reporting my truck had been stolen, I then had the embarrassing task of explaining to the police officer, who had been called to the scene to investigate a serious felony, the nature of my grievous mistake. As a result of this experience, it is my opinion that a sense of humor should be one of the requirements of any job in law enforcement. Seriously, one of these days they will be old and will probably be guilty of something far worse. In my humble opinion, the practice of numbering the aisles in huge parking lots ranks right up there with the greatest ideas of all time.

While embarrassing, this was nothing compared to a humiliating faux pas committed by my friend Billy. Incredible as it may sound, he was actually guilty of attempting to buy a camper which already belonged to him. This rather odd statement requires some explanation. We were camping buddies and spent many enjoyable days and nights camping and sitting around a camp fire drinking bad coffee, playing music, and spinning tall tales. On this particular day, my friend Billy had taken his own camper to the local dealer to have some work done on it. He was directed to the back lot and told to park his camper among several used recreational vehicles the dealer had taken in trade for new ones. Several weeks prior to this day, Billy had been asked by another fellow to be on the lookout for a good, used camper as he was in the market for one. After dropping his trailer in the back lot, Billy went into the office to explain what type work he wanted done with his camper. At this point, he told the salesman who had helped him in the back lot that he was looking to steer one of his friends to a good used camper and wanted to look over what was available. The salesman, sensing a commission in the making, told Billy he had several out back, and they went out too look. My friend perused several before he came to one he really liked. He told the salesman he thought his friend would be interested in that particular model and asked the price, to which he was told, "Why, Mr. Heard, that's the camper you just brought in for us to service." Now, many people would have been too embarrassed to tell this story but not my friend Billy. He repeated this tale around campfires for many years. The world lost a great human when my friend, Billy Heard, passed away, and I still miss him a whole lot.

Now, back to the topic of getting lost: I have been lost on foot in big cities and while hunting in the woods. The difference is that on foot I can still become lost but much more slowly than while driving. It is also possible when lost afoot to simply turn around and go back the way I came in. However, this in not always possible while driving due to the close proximity of many other automobiles traveling at a high rate of speed. Also, the annoying presence of one-way streets prevents the immediate about-face of an automobile, which only makes one even more lost. Making the wrong choice on an interstate has frequently carried me miles from my destination before I was finally able to turn around. In less than a minute an automobile can whisk me to an unknown world from which it usually takes hours to extricate myself.

The laws of chance are generally such that if given the choice of taking a left turn or a right turn, one has at least a fifty-fifty chance of making the correct decision, even if the driver is totally clueless as to which is the correct way to go. This begs the question as to why I make the wrong choice one hundred percent of the time. It would be easier to defy the law of gravity than it would be to change these odds.

A few years back our son and his family lived in Northern Kentucky, right across the river from Cincinnati. Margo and I were traveling to visit them and made one of the myriad stops we are forced to make when on the road for more than twenty minutes. My brain constantly calls out for more coffee while my bladder threatens to get relief one way or the other. Driving a vehicle while simultaneously sipping from a cup of coffee is a way of life, for me but it can become problematic. Apparently, Margo has a bladder made of cast iron and mine is something like a flimsy balloon found at a kid's birthday party fully capable of exploding at any moment. This medical oddity has resulted in her spending several years of her life waiting in the car while I am in the closest restroom. Be that as it may, we had pulled into a rest area after crossing from Tennessee into Kentucky and I had visited today's version of the outhouse. Making our way back to the interstate, we merrily resumed our journey northward, or at least that is what we thought. After traveling several miles we happened upon a roadside sign which indicated that Nashville was only a few miles ahead. This was quite a shock to us, because we had passed through Nashville much earlier on our way north and should have been headed in the opposite direction. Sadly, coming out of the rest area I had somehow taken the wrong turn and headed back south, the way we had come in. It seems impossible but it has happened more than once, even though our car has a compass built into the dash. If Daniel Boone had my sense of direction, Kentucky would have never been settled. Logically, by nothing more than chance, I should occasionally make the right choice but it rarely happens. The same is true when exiting a building with double doors and, for some strange reason one of them is always locked. Inevitably, I always choose the locked side as I attempt to exit the building.

Unlike many folks, Margo and I have never been intrigued with driving to Florida and soaking up the sun. The only attraction for us is the seafood but we can buy that at Captain D's. This particular DNA was apparently lost on our children because they take this trip south frequently and actually seem to enjoy it. There is no doubt that our daughter would gladly give up a professional career if she could just get a job selling t-shirts on the beach.

However, one of my older brothers was in the Navy several years ago and stationed in Key West, Florida. He invited us down for a visit and we felt our kids, who were very young at the time, should have this opportunity to see the Gulf of Mexico and the Atlantic Ocean. Since we had no money to finance such a trip, we made the strange decision to sell the air conditioner out of our house. This decision was made even stranger because it was June and we were headed into the hottest part of the year in North Alabama. We decided to worry about that particular problem when we returned home. Our only reliable vehicle at the time was a small, compact Dodge Omni. This car was very economical on gas, mainly because it was equipped with a four speed transmission, which required constant shifting, and had no air conditioner. By the time we reached South Florida, we were in a pretty miserable state. This particular vehicle was definitely not intended to carry four people and their luggage into a tropical climate which is less than 100 miles from Cuba. To the best of my memory, we did not get lost one single time. One contributing factor was that once we cleared Miami, there was only one road south and that one ended in Key West. To my family's credit, they are able to look back on that experience and laugh. The laughter did not begin until they were able to move out into a house of their own which was air conditioned.

Another strange phenomenon takes place when lost and forced to ask for directions. Of course, the average American male actually asks for directions about as frequently as Haley's Comet comes around the earth, which is about once every seventy years. In addition to creating marital problems, this peculiar male behavior undoubtedly contributes to millions of gallons of gasoline being wasted annually by men who continue to drive around in circles while maintaining they are not lost. One of my brothers once drove to Atlanta to take his family to a Braves game. He could see the stadium from the interstate but could not find the correct exit. Instead of asking for directions to the stadium, he made the decision to turn around and drive all the way back home. Not only did he spend about twelve hours on the round trip, his poor children were distraught because they were huge Braves fans. Immense amounts of tax dollars have been spent studying this strange behavior and it is not my intent to add anything substantive to answer the question, "Why?" No one seems to know why, and the answer may have something to do with testosterone.

My simple observation is that when I do humble myself and ask for directions, I always choose someone who is obviously as lost as I am. An example occurred a few years ago when I was spending a lot of time in Montgomery with absolutely nothing positive to show for it. The same could be said about the legislature of our fine state as this august body has spent much of the last two hundred years doing the same thing. Anyway, I was searching for a specific building on the campus of Alabama State University where I was to attend a meeting of the Society of Lost Causes, or something like that. After driving around for way too long, I spotted a man and woman standing beside a dilapidated pickup truck parked on the side of the street. They were both well along in years and dressed in a manner which suggested they lived in a much more rural area than downtown Montgomery. I pulled alongside them and asked if they could give me directions to my destination. The lady's response was classic, and it often describes my own situation. She said, "Lord no, honey, we're from Red Level and we don't know nothing." Obviously, she intended to convey to me that since they were from another town, they were not familiar with the individual buildings in the neighborhood. The town of Red Level consists of approximately 500 hardy souls and is located in Covington County, which is in Southeastern Alabama not far from the states of Georgia and Florida. Other notable towns in the county include the cities of Opp and Babbie. Her frank response to my question probably did not reflect the sentiment of the Red Level Chamber of Commerce, but her honesty was refreshing.

On many occasions I have been victimized by folks who somehow knew even less than I did about how to get to a certain location, but this minor technicality never fazed them. If Lewis and Clark had asked some of these people for directions they would have wound up in Georgia instead of the west coast. Obviously, people who don't know where they are going should make it a policy never to give directions to others who are equally ignorant of their whereabouts.

Driving a rental vehicle in a large, heavily congested city can cause my brain neurons to make connections they would not normally make while driving my own truck on familiar territory. Margo and I had the privilege of traveling to Hawaii a few years ago and found ourselves with several hours to kill before leaving Honolulu to return home. Not wishing to waste even a few hours in paradise, we rented a car and began driving along the highway, which skirts the perimeter of the island of Oahu. Along the way, we saw huge fields of pineapple and giant waves along the northern coast, which had to measure thirty to forty feet high. We then crossed over Diamondhead as we were about to re-enter Honolulu. There we were treated to a view of the city and Pearl Harbor at twilight often found only on tourist brochures. However, time was getting short as we had to return the rental car and catch a taxi back to the hotel to retrieve our luggage before the shuttle ride to the airport. Downtown Honolulu is a lot like downtown New York City. In the very heart of the city, it is impossible to tell you are on an island in the middle of the Pacific Ocean. The tall buildings, city noise, and congested traffic are no different. It was not difficult at all to spot our destination: the large Hertz sign atop a very tall building. The problem was in figuring out the one-way streets in order to park the car and turn it in. No matter which way I turned, the building was always at least one block away. I felt like a rat in a maze with the clock ticking. One minute the sign was on my right, and the next time it was on my left. We seemed to be playing a game of chase and I was losing.

A hard lesson to learn in life is that there comes a time when we have to realize the way we have been doing things simply does not work, and another plan of action is necessary. It has been said that to continue to make the same mistake over and over while expecting a different result each time is a sure sign of a mental problem. Just because I'm not paranoid doesn't mean they're not out to get me. This axiom was amply demonstrated by the few dullards I foolishly asked for directions.

This was one of those times it was necessary to think outside the box, so to speak. There was one certainty in this cat-and-mouse game and that was we had to be at the airport on time to catch the plane. Somehow I knew American Airlines would not delay departure of a huge 747 while we wandered around downtown Honolulu. Taking the bull by the horns, I parked the car as close as I could possibly get and we walked about two blocks to the Hertz office. The clerk behind the counter was not involved in planning the layout of the one-way streets in the city, nor could he be held accountable for my faulty sense of direction. However, I must not have been the first bump-kin from Alabama he had encountered on the job because he showed no surprise after listening to my dilemma. Hopefully, he was able to locate the car because I never received a bill to pay for a vehicle that was not returned.

Hertz was such an accommodating company with a very liberal return policy, I rented another car from them on a later trip to San Francisco. Surprisingly, they did not have my picture posted behind the counter indicating my business was not welcome because of past indiscretions, such as losing one of their vehicles in downtown Honolulu. The clerk seemed taken aback when I asked, in jest of course, if the exorbitant insurance I had just purchased covered the cost of a new car if I happened to lose the one I had just rented. We had already signed the papers and paid the amount due in advance, so we quickly drove away before he recovered his wits and initiated a background check.

This time our goal was to drive across the Golden Gate Bridge and see as much of the country as possible before return-ing home. Chiefly, we were interested in visiting the Napa Valley region and some of the huge redwoods for which this region is famous. The Napa Valley area of California is world famous for fine, vintage wines produced from grapes grown on the ideally suited soil of that area. Needless to say, the wines are much more expensive and intended for a far different group of folks than those of my native northwest Alabama. Folks around the house generally make do with wine produced from the very common elderberry bushes found growing alongside most dirt roads of the community. On the extremely rare occasion they feel a need for really fine wine, they purchase a bottle of Ripple at the liquor store. Since the homemade wine is stored and drank directly from wide-mouth Mason jars, they are also spared the expense of having to purchase sets of dainty wine glasses favored by the culturally elite.

My only experience with redwoods was the postcard with the picture of one of the huge giants with a tunnel cut through it large enough for a car to pass through. The trip through Napa Valley went well, and our excursion was routine and uneventful until we began searching for the magnificent redwood trees. We were attempting to locate the Muir Woods, which had been designated a national monument. This old growth of coastal redwoods was located only a few miles north of San Francisco. These giants can only be found in Northern California and Southern Oregon. They thrive only in cool coastal regions with a high annual rainfall. John Muir was a noted naturalist and conservationist who had devoted considerable time and energy to saving the giant redwoods from being converted into lumber by the logging industry. It is highly possible that Muir was not involved in cutting the famous tunnel through the aforementioned tree. To my simple way of thinking, this seemed to be in total contradiction to staunch conservationist beliefs and would be frowned upon by tree-huggers world-wide. People who are strongly involved with preserving any type of tree would never hack a tunnel through its trunk.

Our leisure excursion deviated from being sort of ordinary when we began the descent from the elevated plateau into the quiet cove, which had served as a protective sanctuary for the trees for maybe thousands of years. The approach road can be described with three words: narrow, steep, and winding. Our rental car was a small economy size Dodge with an automatic transmission.

There was no way to use the gears to slow the car coming down the steep hill, so it was necessary to stay on the brake until we reached the bottom. About half-way down into the deep gorge we began to detect a rather strong smell which we attributed to the local plant life. I think maybe I suggested it could possibly have been something like Eucalyptus bushes growing on the steep cliff walls. Actually, it could have been a dead whale washed up on the beach for all I knew, since I was taking a wild guess and knew absolutely nothing about Eucalyptus bushes. We soon discovered it was not plant or animal life, dead or alive. It was the smell created when brake shoes become so hot from constant pressure they cause the tires to smoke and threaten to go up in flames. This was brought to our attention when we reached the crowded parking lot at the base of the steep gorge. I made the mistake of taking the first available parking place which was adjacent to a tour bus. The bus had just unloaded a large crowd of Japanese tourists who seemed intent and excited about viewing the giant redwoods. Their attention quickly shifted to us as they began shouting and pointing in our direction. Since Japanese, as well as proper English, is a foreign language to me, I could not figure out exactly what they were saying, but I could tell they were highly agitated. Most were shouting something akin to "kaji, kaji," which I later learned can be loosely translated to mean, "something burning out of control." My bungling abuse of the brakes on the little rental car had apparently turned it into a potential fireball. A few more degrees and we could have conceivably destroyed national treasures, which were probably saplings when Columbus mistakenly thought he had arrived in India and began referring to the folks already here by the wrong name. Some of the giant trees in the grove measured well over 250 feet in height and were completely awe inspiring. We learned that trees in the neighborhood of 350 feet tall could be found much farther north. The large poplars around home were matchsticks compared to these goliaths.

One thing was absolutely for certain, we had to get away from the mob of Japanese tourists. They seemed fixated on us and continued to snap our photos as we strolled around. We weren't sure how they viewed us, but the pictures could definitely be used against us later if we were charged with arson and destruction of a national forest. No wonder celebrities consider the paparazzi to be so annoying. As soon as possible, we casually made our way back to the parking lot and out of the redwood grove, like criminals fleeing the scene of a crime. We felt much more secure and enjoyed the anonymity provided by the masses of people in the city of San Francisco where no one knew about the terrible deed we almost inadvertently committed.

Probably the very worst automobile trip of my life was to Kansas City, Missouri. I already had a plane ticket, which would have taken me a mere three hours from my home to my destination. For reasons still unclear to me, I allowed a friend from Tuscaloosa to talk me into traveling with him in his car on a trip, that consumed one day each way. He arrived at my house about mid-morning on a very hot July day. We were traveling in a mini-van of some kind which provided a lot of room for the two of us and our luggage. The plan was to drive in shifts of two to three hours each with the person not driving having the option of taking a nap in the back. The first hint of trouble came during my driving shift while crossing the Mississippi River near St. Louis. It has always been a habit of mine to take at least a cursory look at the gauges anytime I am behind the wheel. They were put there for a reason. Unfortunately, we were right in the middle of the bridge surrounded by heavy traffic when I noticed the temperature gauge was way to the right of what it should have been. After we had reached the other side and pulled over, my friend volunteered a critical piece of information, which I wished he had shared a lot earlier. As we stood with the hood raised and steam gushing from the radiator, he casually mentioned his car had been running kind of hot lately. This little tidbit would have been extremely valuable when I was pondering much earlier whether or not to take the road trip or the friendly skies to the far side of Missouri. Be that as it may, we managed to limp across the entire state by making frequent stops to water the car.

The car sat in a parking deck most of the time we were in Kansas City, because our hotel was very close to the convention center where we were meeting. However, there was one noteworthy side trip we took to Royals Stadium to watch the local team square off against the New York Yankees. Since we were in Kansas City, and Bo Jackson was in the midst of his historic attempt to play major league baseball with the Royals and professional football with the Oakland Raiders, we figured it would be worth the effort to go out to the ballpark and watch the Alabama native, though an Auburn graduate—and even cheer him on if necessary. Instead of witnessing Bo propel a towering home run out of the park, our efforts were rewarded by watching Bo strike out four times. It was a pleasant night for baseball, and everything went well until we attempted to start the van and leave the parking lot. The battery was as 'dead as a doornail' as we used to say. Thank goodness the folks at the stadium knew from experience that anytime several thousand people are assembled in one place, there will be problems. It is only human nature. Soon, after a boost from a guy patrolling the enormous parking lot in a truck equipped to help folks like us, we were on our way back to the hotel. Omens kept bouncing off me like mosquitoes, and we should have known the trip back home would be anything but peaceful.

Being mostly out of sight and out of mind, we sort of forgot about our earlier troubles with the van, and we looked forward to getting back home. About four days later we were on the road headed home, when our troubles began anew and involved more than an over-heated radiator. For some reason, my friend wanted to take a different route home. It made no difference to me, as long as the road taken led back to North Alabama. We were traveling sort of diagonally across Missouri, and I was driving when the steering wheel became very difficult to turn. Fortunately, we were able to pull into a little crossroads of a community called Hillbilly Junction. Somehow, that name is etched forever into my brain. It was quite obvious something was amiss with the steering. My knowledge of automobile anatomy was very elementary and about on par with what I knew about brain surgery. But even I knew this was a dangerous situation and the car could not be driven in its current condition. Giving credit to my friend where it is due, he crawled under the front of the car and discovered a nut was missing from one of the steering arms, which allowed the left front wheel to turn. Simultaneously, both of us recalled a few miles back when we were sort of startled by something hitting the underside of the car. At the time we figured it was a rock and paid no particular attention to it. Now, we realized it was probably the nut in question. Since I make it a point to keep my AAA membership fully paid up, my solution was to call for a tow truck and take it someplace for a repair. Instead, my friend said he remembered where we lost the nut and was certain he could find it. Before I could remind him that was insane, he had hitched a ride back down the road and left me sitting at a convenience store in Hillbilly Junction, Missouri, with a very bleak outlook on when I might once again see the friendly hills of northwest Alabama.

This quiet time alone gave me an opportunity to recall an event back down the road, which probably explained why the nut came loose in the first place. Asleep in the back seat, I was abruptly awakened by the vehicle bouncing along on extremely uneven ground. To my horror, I discovered my stupid friend was in the process of chasing a coyote across a large tract of almost flat land adjacent to the highway. The coyote had crossed the highway in front of the van, and suddenly, we were in hot pursuit. The madman behind the wheel was stymied when the wily coyote leaped a ditch, and he was forced to admit defeat. Needless to say, the front end of a mini-van is not built like a tank, and there was no telling what other damage had been done.

Patience has never been one of my strong points. My wife will attest long and loud to this fact. As I sat waiting, I began to plan out my escape from Hillbilly Junction, Missouri (it could have been Arkansas). My sanctuary served as the focal point of the community. It was a gas station, convenience store, post office, and bus stop. The bus stop part was of particular interest because it afforded me a way out. If I could only get to Memphis, I was fairly certain I could persuade Margo to come and pick me up. While standing in line to inquire about the bus schedule, a miracle occurred. My friend arrived, having hitched a ride back, and as incredible as it may sound, he was holding the prized nut in his hand. Yes, somehow he had managed to find the proverbial needle in a haystack. At that point, we should have made a beeline to the closest casino. With his kind of luck, he could have cleaned out every slot machine in the joint. Instead, we borrowed a wrench, replaced the nut, and headed south.

This story should have had a happy ending after this close encounter with disaster, but it actually got worse. Fixing the steering problem did nothing to solve the hot radiator problem which had plagued us since leaving home days ago. My friend was behind the wheel when we pulled into a service station of sorts, in West Memphis, Arkansas. A fellow wearing what passed for a mechanics outfit decreed we had a thermostat problem, which was causing the radiator to over-heat. He assured us that his able assistant, Chigger, could run down the road to the parts store and return in a few minutes with a new thermostat, which would solve all our problems. About two hours later, Chigger did return but with the sad news there was no thermostat to be found anywhere in West Memphis that would fit this particular vehicle. It has been written that in ancient times, the bearer of bad news was often killed. However, by this time my spirit had been broken by bad news followed by more bad news, and I was simply not up to the task. As a result, Chigger was allowed to live another day. Unhappily, more bad news was to follow.

The wannabe mechanic did offer some advice, which sounded kind of plausible to our desperate ears. His reasoning was that the heat from the engine was not being vented properly through the cooling system because of a faulty thermostat. Furthermore, over the years he had heard a possible temporary solution to the problem would be to turn the heater up full blast which would convey the heat from the engine block to the inside of the vehicle. On a frigid day in mid-February this would have been an excellent idea, but on a scalding hot day in July in the Deep South it might prove to be a mite uncomfortable. However, as they say, desperation is the mother of invention, so we took to the road with hot air coming from the heater vents and in through all the windows. Before departing Memphis, we did stop at a super market and purchase a case of Perrier bottled water and two bags of ice. The radiator consumed more of the Perrier than we did, but by placing the bag of ice on top of our head we were able to ward off a heat stroke, but just barely. Thankfully, my fear of trying to explain to a Mississippi deputy sheriff why we were driving with the heater on in July and bags of ice on our head never materialized. This unfortunate occurrence would have surely necessitated an overnight stay in a jail cell, while local authorities checked with mental institutions to determine if any residents had turned up missing.

We were able to eventually make it to my house, although in miserable condition. Margo has scolded me for years because I did not invite my friend to spend the night before going on to Tuscaloosa. Frankly, I had endured all of him I could stand over the last several days. In addition, by the time we got back to the house he was no longer my friend, therefore we had no obligation to provide lodging for the night. The unbearable heat inside his van had melted away any bonds of friendship which had survived the coyote incident. This simple fact alone alleviated any feelings of guilt I might otherwise have felt. As the tail lights of his minivan disappeared down my driveway, I felt like weeping for joy. Needless to say, our friendship never recovered to the point of attempting another road trip together.

The calamitous road trip to Missouri was only the tip of the iceberg when it comes to my experience with undependable vehicles. Being lost is bad enough but being left stranded is even worse. This has happened to me both near home and far away, with the latter definitely being the worse of the two evils.

Probably the most undependable vehicle I have ever owned was a black, one-half ton, Dodge pickup truck. It left the assembly plant with a four speed floor shift but had the equivalent of a gender change later in life. At the time, I had to spend considerable time out of town attending fruitless meetings all across the state, and it was much more convenient for me to take our small car which was a lot better on gas. This left Margo to drive a truck, which required the use of her right arm to constantly shift gears. She found this very annoying, because her right arm was needed to keep our two children upright on the bench seat beside her. At the time, seat belts were not required, and most children were kept from crashing into the front windshield by the rigid right arm of a parent who was also heavily involved at the time with driving the vehicle. This made shifting gears a lower priority for Margo, and she demanded a change. As a matter of fact, she put it another way. I believe she said if I didn't do something about the @#$%^ truck, she would push it off into Cypress Creek. Her threat to take action was taken quite seriously, because the creek conveniently flowed only a few feet from our house. Even more conveniently, our house was on a hill above the creek and virtually no effort would be required on her part to make it happen. Urged on by this threat, I visited a local transmission shop, and they purged the truck of the manual shift and installed an automatic transmission in its place. This made it easier for Margo to keep our children's heads out of the windshield and hard metal dash but did nothing to make the truck more dependable.

The fact that the old manual transmission was no longer installed in our truck did not mean it no longer tormented

Margo. Since it was a perfectly good transmission, I could not force myself to take it to the dump as she insisted. It remained at our house for about five more years until we moved. It accompanied us to our new home, where it languished in the basement for ten more years. During this entire time, I was forced to listen to her claim that nobody would ever want that hideous hunk of metal. On a whim one day, as I was experimenting with listing unwanted items to sell on Craigslist, the transmission came to mind. Within three hours of being listed, it was sold to a fellow from across the state line in Mississippi for one hundred dollars. He got a bargain and I got vindication.

Occasionally, I was called upon to go to our nation's capital in order to attend fruitless meetings and soon grew tired of airports and airplanes. Having flown so much I figured the laws of chance were closing in on me, and every successful flight increased the risk of the next one being unsuccessful. I had loved trains since childhood so I began traveling to Birmingham and rode the rails overnight to Washington. It did not make sense to leave Margo's car in a parking deck for a week at a time, so I made plans to take my truck. Before leaving, I loaded the truck with every conceivable item I would need when it had its inevitable break down. The most valuable piece of information was the phone number for AAA. As a matter of fact, I was on a first name basis with their emergency service operator responsible for dispatching tow trucks to customers with vehicles like mine. Cullman had been designated as my predetermined point of no return. If the breakdown occurred before I reached Cullman, I would call AAA and return home. Beyond that point, I would sort of play it by ear. Surprisingly enough, I made it all the way to the parking deck across the street from the train depot in downtown Birmingham before disaster struck. I had actually pulled into a parking place and congratulated myself on the successful trip, when I made the mistake of backing out to straighten up and the engine died. The engine fluttered to a halt and would not make a sound as I desperately tried to re-start it. My parking spot was on an incline and the truck quit right smack in the middle of the up and down ramp between the different levels. I quickly consulted the attendant and then called AAA. Naturally, they arrived at the wrong entrance and sat there as precious minutes wasted away before they were finally directed to the right door. At that point, it was apparent they had mistakenly brought the truck they used to jump-start low batteries, so they had to go back and get the tow truck. About this time was when I made the decision to do something totally out of character for me. I trusted the attendant to take care of the situation, because the train was about to leave the station in a very real sense. The New Orleans to New York Amtrak was on an elevated platform, and from my small compartment I could see the parking deck, which was just right across the street. With what could only be described as mixed feelings, I watched as the tow truck emerged with my black Dodge trailing obediently behind it. The thought did cross my mind that with good luck maybe I would never see it again.

My faith in human nature was restored about a week later after collecting my luggage and walking across the street. The trusty attendant was right where he said he would be. We left the deck in his car and traveled to the west side of the city near Legion Field where the truck had been taken, at his direction, to be repaired. We were happily reunited and after paying a hefty repair bill and an equally hefty tip for the helpful attendant, I headed back toward the house and, miraculously, made the entire trip home without further incident. Not long after the incident at the train station, the old black Dodge was traded for a used Silverado with an automatic transmission and seat belts. We decided to follow the advice of Dinah Shore and "see the USA in our Chevrolet."

There is no doubt that Americans have long had a love-hate relationship with their automobiles. We look for different things in our cars, much as we do with the people in our life. Unfortunately, being sleek, fast, and good-looking is not the same as being dependable--in people or automobiles. At one time, owning a Corvette would have been the high point of my shallow existence, but time changes things, hopefully for the better. A shiny Corvette sitting in the yard may look good, but if it won't start, it will never get me to Wal-Mart. Many times I have allowed my frustration to get the best of me when my car or truck wouldn't run, needed tires, or expensive repairs. All-in-all, today's vehicles are much more comfortable and dependable than those of our parents. If only they could be made to look as classy as those from the '50s and '60s, it would be a classic case of having our cake and eating it too.

Life without automobiles can be seen only a few miles north of my home at a community of Amish people. They often have to go to Wal-Mart like the rest of us but first have to fetch the horse from the pasture, put on the harness, and then hitch the horse to the buggy. All of this preparation precedes a long and often, very cold, or hot, trip to town.

We are often guilty of telling the younger generation that they have it made. So do most of the rest of us, but we just won't admit it.

******

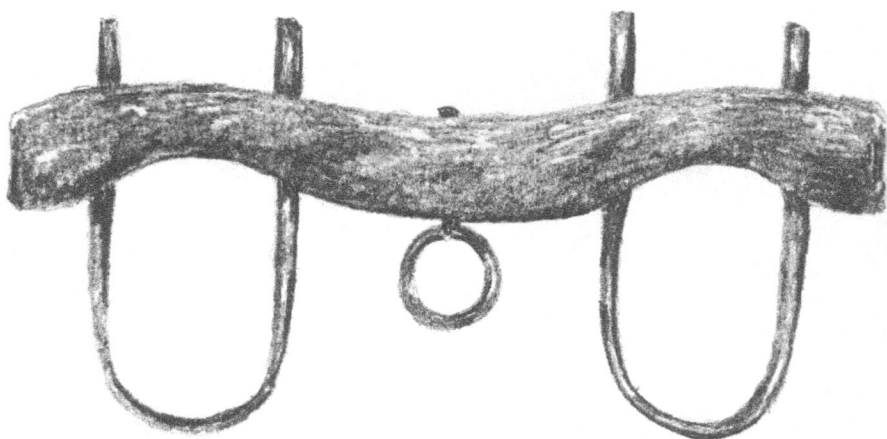

Jackie Hastings

Conquer the Clutter

My life has been full of surprises, particularly as I have gotten older. When I finally manage to get my brain into passing gear, my body feels like the clutch and transmission fell out way back down the road, which means I am only coasting. Sadly, coasting works well only when you're headed downhill, and after every downhill there is usually another hill to climb. That's why I had to give up riding a bicycle. That is just the way life is! But the older I get there is an occasional gem to stumble over. I find that there is really not that much worth waiting in line for, which offers some consolation.

Nowadays, I find myself being wrong about more things than I would have thought possible in my younger years. Hindsight tells me that I was wrong a lot even back then but wasn't smart enough to know it. The few times I knew I was wrong, I wouldn't admit it. This realization has not only startled me but has also brought about a lot of anguish. Eating crow is bad enough when it is straight out of the oven but becomes a lot worse when it is served cold as a leftover. However, if one eats enough cold crow, everything else that might come along down the road looks and tastes a whole lot better. Statistics show that I am right less than half the time, but it does trouble me a little bit that my wife keeps all the statistics at our house. She works strictly from memory and never allows me to see the actual numbers, which proves she is a lot smarter than me.

One of the real surprises about growing old is the amount of clutter I have managed to accumulate over the years. For some reason, I thought as I got older life would become simpler and less complicated, but, man, have I been wrong! Living in the same place a long time allows most of us to collect far too much stuff. We know we can't take it with us, but it sure is hard to learn from our mistakes. Living without a lot of stuff can be done but takes a heap of discipline. For proof, just ask anyone who moves frequently, like career military veterans and Methodist ministers. A moving van is a big part of their lives.

However, since most of us do not fit into either category, a great deal of self-discipline is necessary. In a sense, our property holds us hostage. The more stuff we have, the longer it takes to look after it. Personally, there are times when my wife and I have failed to go somewhere or take a trip simply because we felt we had to be around the house to look after stuff, whether it was livestock, pets, or other things. We don't have to be inside a jail cell to be a prisoner.

Sometimes, we feel we have to accumulate the most ridiculous items. My daddy was notorious for not throwing anything away. As a matter of fact, he would take home things other people intended to throw away, thinking he would eventually find a use for it. An example would be gallon plastic milk cartons. He saved them as if they were gold plated and hung them like giant clusters of grapes from the rafters in his barn. He reasoned they would come in handy when he went jug fishing. If he had used only a portion of them for this purpose, they would have clogged the main channel of the Tennessee River from Wright to Waterloo. During the forty-five years of my life that I knew him, he may have gone jug fishing no more than two or three times.

The clutter we allow in our lives may present a physical problem for us, but it is actually a mental one. The decision to jettison the things in life that have become a heavy burden is not an easy one and is very difficult to make. It is also difficult to actually do the deed after you have made the decision. There have been times when I finally found the will to dispose of something, only to change my mind and retrieve it from the trash can. The clutter was hard to live with, but the real question was: could I live without it? I have come to believe that most of us are more comfortable living with a known misery than having to make a change which might, or might not, bring some relief. Bad things are generally in store for folks who make the same mistakes over and over again and expect a different result each time. If we look up and find ourselves still using carbon paper while living in a world which runs on computers, it might be a good idea to consider changing some of our ways. At least, we ought to get rid of the carbon paper. Maybe change is so difficult, because it introduces an unknown element into our lives, and that is what frightens us the most.

There comes a time in all our lives when we have to dispose of the clutter we have allowed to accumulate around us. People use a variety of methods to dispose of clutter, but some folks never seem to get around to it. There is the story of an old fellow who once lived in our community who had collected so much stuff he was relieved when his house caught fire. That may or may not be true, but most everybody I know keeps a burn pile somewhere around their place. Maybe that revelation in itself suggests I should consider looking for a better class of friends. For the uninitiated, a burn pile is a collection of debris, accumulated over a period of time that is gradually piled somewhere out back and set ablaze when the time is right. Pity the poor folks who live in neighborhoods which prohibit burning anything outside. The only qualification necessary to be a part of the pile is the items have to be flammable and to have reached a point of no return as far as usefulness is concerned. You don't want items on the pile which will not burn. Otherwise, you will create another unsightly mess which will have to be dealt with all over again in an entirely different way.

The theory behind a burn pile, to my way of thinking, is to get rid of items which are no longer needed. That is the crux of the problem for most of us: to decide when we no longer need an item. It takes a great deal of courage to toss certain items on the burn pile. We tend to hang on to possessions, thinking we may need them somewhere down the road. Sometimes that road does not have an end: it just keeps on going. Maybe the best time to actually toss certain objects on the pile is when you already have the fire going. That would prevent us from changing our mind and reclaiming what we tried to throw away. There is a real danger of being burned if we aren't real careful.

There can be a great deal of satisfaction watching a pile of unneeded and unwanted items go up in flames. It generally takes a good while to accumulate a pile, and it can become quite an eyesore. That is the main reason the pile should be kept out behind the house. As a matter of fact, some piles take most of a lifetime to get to the point when we realize it is time they have to go, but the sooner we can get around to disposing of it, the better off we are. Some folks have been known to borrow some of their neighbor's clutter and add it to their own pile in an effort to get the process under way sooner.

After the fire is out, the only left-over evidence should be a pile of ashes. It is a matter of pride with me to reduce a huge pile of debris to a pile which can be scattered, and when the grass grows back there is no evidence the pile ever existed. My burn piles consist mostly of limbs picked up over time, particularly after windy days. However, I have been known to throw broken furniture and scrap wood and cardboard packaging onto the pile. A real hot fire will burn most anything. City folk may not be familiar with the idea of maintaining a burn pile to dispose of clutter. Burning is frowned upon when there are a lot of neighbors nearby. This is probably a good thing in that we should be mindful not to burn down our neighbor's house while trying to clean up the clutter in our own life. It could be that there is only a fine line separating people who keep a burn pile from arsonists.

I remember when a handy ditch out behind the house served the same purpose as a good burn pile and was actually more inclusive. All the unwanted clutter around the place was tossed into the ditch, and being flammable was not a prerequisite. Growing up, we tossed bed springs, worn out tires, old stoves, and literally tons of inflammable items in a ditch solely because there was nowhere else to put them. This was sort of an out of sight, out of mind policy. If the ditch was far enough from the house, no one ever knew it was there.

The same principle applies to the clothesline. It must always be in back of the house. No respectable person hangs their underwear in front of the house where everyone can see. Momma always said not to throw our stuff away and leave it in plain sight. When that happens, others are prone to go through it. A lot can be found out about a person by going through the clutter in their lives. Archaeologists consider it a gold mine to discover mounds and caves where those folks who lived there before us simply kept piling up stuff and lived right on top of it. They were not much different from us. The only way to get rid of all the clutter they had accumulated was to bury it. Their entire history could be uncovered by digging through what was once their trash. We should make it a point of emphasis never to live our lives in the middle of a pile of garbage! This could be a rather simple explanation of why some civilizations no longer exist. It may be necessary to visit the garbage dump occasionally, but don't stay long enough to be considered a resident. There is a big difference.

The clutter which we allow to accumulate around us can sometimes be rendered meaningless in a matter of a split second. Countless hours of labor and collecting stuff for a singular purpose can disappear faster than a casserole at a gathering of Methodists. A good friend once asked me if I had spent any time puttering around the creek bottom below our house. I responded that, yes, I spent a lot of time sort of exploring and observing whatever might be in the vicinity. Specifically, he asked if I had spent any time on the other side of the creek. Since this property did not belong to us, I replied that I had been on the other side of the creek but had not spent much time there.

My friend went on to relay a rather humorous story about an incident which had occurred on the creek bank across from our house. It seems that when he was a very young man, a friend of his suggested they could make some good money by cooking up a little liquor, and he had the perfect spot already picked out. His father owned quite a bit of land in a very secluded area in West Lauderdale County which had a creek flowing through it. An isolated spot with plenty of fresh, clear water was ideal for what they had in mind. Now, connoisseurs of fine moonshine liquor know that fresh water is one of the essential ingredients for the production of what some call moonshine, white lightning, corn liquor, bootleg liquor, hooch, shine, mountain dew, or home brew. Some even refer to it as bathtub gin. Whatever the name, it is highly illegal and many have spent considerable time behind bars for cluttering up the community and their lives with the tools necessary for the job. In addition to fresh water, another key ingredient for the successful pursuit of this endeavor is secrecy. However, it is always dangerous to allow yourself to believe others will keep your secret. Someone once said for three people to keep a secret, two of them have to be dead.

When it was all said and done, my friend, being unemployed at the moment and with few prospects for gainful employment, concluded that it sounded like a good idea to him. The partnership now secure, they went about their new business with the gusto and enthusiasm that only footloose and fancy free young men could summon. In order to further protect their investment from prying eyes, they decided to take the time to dig a huge pit in which to hide the various tanks, coils and other assorted paraphernalia needed to squeeze some liquid gold from a few bushels of corn. Since lawmen were always on the lookout for prohibited enterprises such as this, security was of the utmost importance.

The wily lawmen would check with local grocery stores to see who was buying an unusual amount of sugar. They also showed a great deal of interest in fellows who might be spending a lot of cash money despite not having a job in years.

They spent several days digging the pit and installing their equipment. They took security to an extreme by covering the entire site with rusty metal taken from an old collapsed barn not far from the site. Supposedly, this precaution protected them from an attack from the air. As coincidence would have it, this entire operation took place just a few hundred yards from our present home.

Now, my friend is a very upstanding member of the community and is highly respected by all who are privileged to know him. One might wonder why he would agree to such an enterprise as moonshining. Basically, it was a very simple decision. There were no jobs to be had and southerners by the thousands were leaving the family farm and heading north to Ohio, Illinois, Indiana, and Michigan to work in the big factories. Good paying jobs were available in the automobile and steel industries. It sure beat cutting timber and pulpwood in North Alabama, and, to tell the truth, many of their neighbors generally knew what was going on, but being an informant was just not in their blood. It might be added they also enjoyed an occasional snort from the liquor jug.

Before my friend and his buddy could establish themselves in the illegal liquor business, they were sort of "nipped in the bud" as Barney Fife would say. Moonshiners will tell you that their chosen profession involved long hours of hard labor and then long hours of waiting. In spite of taking every precaution they could think of, their hard work was all for naught.

It has been said more than once that mothers seem to have eyes in the back of their heads, and their intuition has never been adequately explained. They seem to have an uncanny knack for knowing when their offspring are up to no good. One hot, summer day as they were waiting out the fermentation process on their first real run of liquor, a funny thing happened. My friend explained to me that he just had a strange feeling he was being watched. Sure enough, he was right! He looked up and not more than fifty feet away stood his friend's mother. He said he nudged his buddy and pointed toward her. To say the least, both of them were speechless. He said the really strange thing was that the old lady did not say a word to either of them. She just stood and watched, taking in the entire operation. Then she just turned and headed back into the woods in the direction of their house. Now, talk about throwing a wrench into the gearbox!

My friend confided that he asked me about the creek bottom because the still was abandoned that very day and he never returned. He did not know what had happened to any of the equipment but had always wondered. As a matter of fact, he lived in fear for weeks that his friend's mother would report them to the county sheriff. Apparently, she kept quiet about what she saw and nothing came from it, except that he had suffered the scare of his life. Well, there was one positive consequence: he straightened out his life and was never again tempted to cross over the line.

I have said a lot to make one small point. My friend was able to walk away from clutter that in all probability would have made his life vastly different. A stint in federal prison can exert a negative influence on future employment opportunities. Not only did he walk away, he never looked back. That is the very best way to treat clutter.

After hearing his tale, curiosity got the best of me and I went down to the creek bottom with one purpose in mind. Yes, I did find evidence of a large depression in the ground with pieces of rusty metal barely visible. There was no doubt this was the site of the moonshine still from long ago. Actually, I had seen the metal many times before from our side of the creek but had attributed it to a collapsed shed or barn. Apparently, spring floods and time had, for all practical purposes, de-cluttered the creek bank.

Ridding our lives of unwanted clutter is not a new phenomenon. It has been going on since the beginning of time. The things we allow to clutter our lives can be more than just physical objects that can be disposed of in a burn pile or a deep ditch. Much of today's clutter involves emotional and even spiritual matters. Without even realizing it, we allow the clutter of resentment, envy, jealousy, job stress, materialism, and hatred to affect our lives in such a way we lose sight of what life should really be all about. We live in an environment that oftentimes shapes our lives in a negative way.

There is a line in one of my favorite hymns, *Lord of the Dance*, which is something to the effect that it is "hard to dance with the devil on your back." Personal experience has proven to me that it is extremely hard to do anything with the devil on your back; which, by the way, is the worst example of clutter a fellow could ever imagine. The problem is that sometimes we don't realize the devil is on our back and we just continue to dance on, stumbling and falling every step of the way, believing all of our problems are a result of being a poor dancer. You see, the devil loves for us to carry him around on our back. That way, it is easier for him to whisper in our ear. If we tote him around long enough we may actually come to believe his lies.

All the while, he is convincing us he does not exist, which is the biggest lie he ever told.

The old adage that you can't judge a book by its cover applies to more than just books. Looking at a person from the outside, they may seem to have the perfect life and everything is in order. They have a nice home, new car, perfect children, and a good job. However, that is often far from the truth of the matter. That car, house, and job stress may be the devil in disguise in the form of materialism. We never really know what is affecting a person on the inside. People carry burdens around with them all their lives and never find the equivalent of a burn pile or ditch to relieve their load. Eventually, the burden becomes too great to carry any longer, and lives fly out of control and people are hurt, mentally and physically. Our world seems to be plagued by addictions of all kinds with many of them being an attempt to relieve our lives of the burdens we have on our back. They provide a temporary reprieve and take us to a place where we no longer feel the pain. The problem is that the reality is still around, and the resulting addiction becomes a disease instead of a cure.

I have promised myself I would rid my life of the clutter that distracts me from what is really important. Items that have been around for years waiting to be used are going to the dump. I know it is hard to let go, but I have to remember that absolutely none of my material possessions will last forever. When we learn to relinquish our grip on worldly things and, instead, turn to eternal things, we will all find ourselves one step closer to what God would have us to be.

I have to be mindful of the fact that much of the real harmful clutter in my life is pride, envy, jealousy, and the wrong-headed habit of placing the worldly ahead of the eternal. It is wonderful to find rest for the body after a day of hard labor. It is even better to find rest for the soul when we finally realize God has provided a burn pile for all our burdens in the form of Jesus

Christ. Christ gives us the only opportunity we will ever have to trade things we will never be able to take with us anyway for something eternal that we will never be able to lose. He tells us in the book of Matthew that, "My yoke is easy to bear, and the burden I give you is light."

Personal experience has taught me beyond a shadow of a doubt that the burden is a lot lighter when we allow Jesus to get the devil off our back.

******

Jackie Hastings

Cutting the Grass

As the years of my life have played out behind me like a broken string of cheap beads scattered in a thousand different directions, I have come across some things which have truly astonished me. Acquaintances and relatives have claimed to enjoy activities which have seemed so perverse to what my daddy claimed was good common sense that I have questioned not only their common sense, but their sanity as well. To avoid emptying the closet of skeletons, I will mention only one: the preposterous claim some folks make that they actually enjoy mowing the yard.

Notice I said "yard" and not the more socially acceptable term "lawn." Where I grew up, most people did not have lawns, they had yards. People who have a lawn probably eat lunch in the middle of the day instead of dinner, and at the end of the day they sit down and enjoy dinner instead of supper. While I am venting, I'll bet a dollar to a doughnut these are the very same folks who turn their children loose at large gatherings where food is served so they can rush to the head of the line. Roosevelt's Rough Riders have nothing on Methodists charging the food table at a church function, and the little children are taught this survival technique very early in life. It is best not to dwell on the knowledge that they are visually inspecting each and every piece of the fried chicken, searching for the elusive drumstick.

Folks my age grew up under a more orderly system. When I was a boy, kids were told to wait until all the adults in the crowd had been through the line and filled their plates before the little urchins engulfed the tables like hogs around a slop bucket. Actually, the kids in the crowd were at the lower end of the pecking order which is where they belong. It is the upper end of that pyramid that was totally out of whack. The men ate first followed by the women. Now, there is absolutely nothing right about that system. The women had slaved for hours cooking the food, and the men came in from the outside where they had spent most of the day hunkering down, spitting, and telling outlandish lies. In my new world, the women would eat first, the men second, and the kids last.

At our family gatherings, my greatest fear was that my uncles and brothers ahead of me would scoop up all the good food and leave nothing but the green Jell-O and chicken necks. This strictly southern social code apparently changed during the decade after I reached the age of thirty. At that point in my life I was too depressed to notice and obviously not paying attention. But, I have said repeatedly that many things from my childhood have changed over the years and nothing remains the same forever. The previous statement is not an admission these changes have been for the betterment of society. It is simply an admission I have accepted the fact that changes have occurred, and it matters not a bit whether or not I happen to agree. To my utter amazement, most changes have taken place without my prior approval. But, let me return to the topic at hand, mowing the yard.

Perhaps my disdain for mowing is a result of the archaic conditions under which I first was given that responsibility. Our old house in East Florence did not have anything resembling a lawn. Instead, we lived in sort of a low place on top of a hill which had little flat ground. The fact of the matter is that we lived in the drainage ditch, which moved water from the top of the hill to the creek bottom below the hill. It wasn't so much that land was scarce and unavailable. It was more like money was scarce and unavailable! What ground there was around our house grew only Johnson grass and rocks. A word to the uninformed might be useful at this juncture. A stalk of Johnson grass is one of the hardest substances known to mankind. Strands of this hardy grass are frequently used to replace steel cables supporting large bridges such as the Golden Gate Bridge near San Francisco, California.

The entire time we lived in that house we never had a grass-cutting machine which had a motor permanently attached. The power came in the form of whichever of my parents' children picked up the device and started swinging it or pushing it. In other words, we had only a sling blade and a push-type reel mower. Thankfully, both have now been banned as hazards to the health and well-being of those assigned to use them. The child experts of today could reasonably argue that this experience scarred me for life. Most people who know me will not argue that point.

For decades my wife, Margo, and I have vowed never to complain about the bugs and the hot humid weather we endure during the summer. Of course, we have always made this vow during the middle of a winter which seemingly will never end. Inevitably, we stand in the living room in February and watch the rain run from the roof and just hope it doesn't turn cold enough to freeze. Our thoughts have long ago turned to summer and the warm balmy breezes we enjoy while sitting on our screened-in back porch sipping cold, iced tea. All is well until it comes time to once again begin the weekly ritual of mowing the yard. This chore forces us to abandon our last bastion of sanity in a world that sometimes seems to have gone stark-raving mad.

Neither of us takes any delight in mowing the yard. It is the equivalent of a root canal without the anesthetic. We prefer sitting on the porch and sipping iced tea and occasionally dozing off in the hammock. Of course, time and invention have made the process somewhat more pleasant. Gone forever are the old sling blade and the reel mower. They have been replaced by fast, sleek riding mowers which can turn on a dime and have a cup holder for my tea glass. Mostly, the horsepower and cutting width are secondary to a cup holder. A mower without a cup holder is worthless in my book. Couple a forty-eight inch cut with a twenty-two horsepower engine and my complaints won't hold much water. This situation works well most of the time until Margo tries to turn her mower into a stump-eater or tries to shred a horseshoe stob into steel filings.

By the way, a stob is what northerners call a stake. It is generally of varying lengths and sharpened on one end and made of either wood or metal. It is driven into the ground to serve a specific purpose. I threw this bit of information in just in case someone north of the Mason-Dixon Line stumbles across one of my books in the one dollar bin outside of a thrift store and needs an interpreter to figure out what I am trying to say.

Sometimes complacency tends to ruin us, and it is good never to forget that any contraption with an internal combustion engine can cause massive heartbreak in a matter of a few seconds. What can be more frustrating than pulling on a rope, hoping to induce a sputter of life from a gas engine which is bound and determined to cause a stroke or a massive coronary? Many vile and unchristian-like words have escaped my lips during these moments. For some reason, every weed-eater, chainsaw, leaf-blower, and lawnmower I have ever owned seems to hold a grudge against me and is determined to create havoc in my life. New-Age people would just say that our vibes are out of line with the stars and moon, but I have discovered I am not alone. Misery loves company or something like that. A friend once buried his push-mower in a large pit in his yard which had been dug for the purpose of installing a grease trap for his home. After pulling the starting rope for far too long, he lost his cool and in a complete rage buried the mower with only the handles protruding ignominiously above the ground as a constant reminder of his hot-headed loss of control. He finally moved to a new home. Fortunately, I had a creek nearby which was the final resting place for many hand-cranked gasoline engines. Thus, we were able to remain in the home we dearly loved.

The day I was able to sit astride our first riding mower is remembered fondly. Now, it was not new and shiny, far from it. Maybe it had once been painted but the evidence was long gone. The entire exterior was either grease or dirt. Actually, I had salvaged it from the front yard of a neighbor who was attempting to load it into the back of his truck to haul it to the county dump. A county dump is sometimes referred to as a land fill, but there is absolutely no difference. It was a Craftsman mower which means it came from Sears. It did not have a traditional steering wheel, but it was steered by handlebars like one finds on a bicycle. The reason the mower was headed for the dump was quite simple: it would not run. Another minor problem was that the last time the engine had actually produced power it had only one forward gear which functioned. When it left the factory many decades before, it had three forward gears but two of them had kicked the bucket due to excessive wear and tear. If it had been equipped with an odometer it would have cycled around at least twice. According to the owner, the only remaining gear produced a forward speed of about five miles per hour. This was very frustrating and caused it to be more time consuming that a push mower. And, one more thing, the reverse gear had joined two of its brethren and gone on to glory. The transmission problems were actually not relevant because, as I said earlier, the engine would not run.

Not one to look a gift horse in the mouth, the old mower was loaded into my truck to be given a new lease on life, hopefully.

My knowledge of the internal combustion engine was very limited at that time, as it continues to be today. It would be highly presumptuous to think anything I did to the mower made it run but run it did. For a million dollars, I could not explain how this miracle occurred. Maybe it had old gas or maybe I was holding my tongue right. I have no idea. Encouraged by my incredibly good luck, I tore into the transmission with absolutely no clue what I was looking for. There was something called a cog, or gear, or something of that nature that did look a little frazzled and worse for the wear. With nothing else to go on, I took this little gizmo to Sears and my lucky streak continued. They actually had one in stock. This has never happened to anyone in the entire history of that company. Every part I have ever needed from Sears had to be ordered from the mountains of Tibet and delivered by monks riding Llamas. Be that as it may, the little doodad was just what the doctor ordered. Not only did the engine run, it would move forward at a reasonable rate of speed with the blade engaged. There was a minor problem with reverse, but who cuts grass going backwards anyway? For the first time in my life, I could sit on a machine and cut grass. Ain't this country wonderful? Goodbye push mower and sling blade!

Little did I realize at the time that this seemingly unbelievable string of good luck would begin a long and bitter relationship between me and riding mowers. Some might call it bad karma or whatever, but there is just something about me that seems to bring out the very worst in an internal combustion engine. The final resting place of the salvaged Craftsman did turn out to be the county dump after all. My efforts to revive the old machine only delayed the inevitable. It went up in flames, literally, on a very hot day in July. Since it was very difficult to start, I usually left the engine running when I had to get off and do something else. On that fateful day in July, I parked it with the engine running and went into the house for a cold glass of sweet tea. When I returned a few minutes later it was fully engulfed in flames. It burned right down to the wheels and there was nothing left but a charred hunk of twisted metal. More times than we know, our fate is often determined by a matter of minutes. A glass of iced, cold tea actually was responsible for saving my life. Thankfully, I had not parked the old machine on the carport.

Shortly after I retired and my wife was still gainfully employed, I had a similar moment with another used mower I had purchased from one of my brothers when he moved back to Virginia. The mower was quite old when I bought it, and it did give us several years of good service. As the years passed it became less and less dependable until the inevitable finally occurred. No amount of innovative words could produce any sign of life from the despicable machine. Vowing to solve the problem once and for all, I jumped into my truck and drove to the Lowe's store in town. I finally had enough of hand-me-down mowers, and it was my intention to purchase a brand spanking new riding mower. This rather rash act was accomplished with the assistance of a credit card but only after giving them a blood sample and some of my DNA. It should be noted here this entire transaction took place without the approval of my wife.

Our house is situated on a hillside, so I drove to the mostly flattened area at the top in front of my shop in order to unload my new purchase. My shop is located above the house and is about one hundred feet higher than the creek bottom below it. A common obstruction to loading and unloading a riding mower from the bed of a pickup truck is the cutting deck which frequently lodges where the tailgate is attached to the truck bed. I made quick work of this obstacle as I jumped into the truck bed and gave the mower a mighty shove and it rolled smoothly and quickly down the ramps to the ground. Unfortunately, it did not stop moving. As I said, I was at the top of a rather steep hill and the mower rapidly picked up speed as it headed down the hill toward the creek bottom. My short legs were no match for the swiftly moving machine, and the realization came quickly that any further chase was futile. My only recourse was to stop and watch as it shot down the hill. Afterwards, I wondered what I could have done had I been able to overtake it. The momentum of several hundred pounds of steel and plastic on four wheels far exceeded my ability to bring it to a screeching halt. It reminded me of the dog chasing a car: what do I do if I catch it? Two questions competed for attention inside my muddled brain. What would my wife say about an expenditure on the north side of a thousand dollars with nothing but broken plastic and smashed steel to show for it? For a fleeting moment I actually tried to think of what I could say to the people at Lowe's if I returned it and asked for a refund. Their return policy is not that liberal and was not intended to cover mowers damaged by smashing into trees while racing backwards down a steep hill. The obvious answer to both questions made me very sad.

However, there is an upside to this story. God has blessed me all my life with more than any one person could ever deserve. On this day, He blessed me one more time. The mower moved backwards at NASCAR-like speed, missing every giant oak and poplar tree purposely left in place to beautify that hillside. After what seemed like an eternity, the mower came to a stop at the bottom of the hill, completely unscathed and none the worse for the experience. Only a Valium-laced salt-lick would have quieted my nerves at the moment. God is good, all the time!

It is difficult for me to admit but mowing the yard is not all bad and can be a time for reflection and contemplation and can sometimes hold surprises no one could predict. One such day a short time ago, I cranked up the old Cub Cadet and had been cutting for only a few minutes when I looked up and saw a strange sight. A young man and a very attractive woman were standing in my yard, and there was no sign of a vehicle anywhere. The fact that there was no vehicle was highly unusual because people just do not walk up to our house unannounced. We live in a very rural area with an extremely long driveway, and pedestrians are very rare under any circumstances. On most occasions our dog announces the arrival of people and machines unless he is being chased by a chipmunk. Trying to be polite without seeming too curious, I drove the mower over and turned off the engine. The conversation went something like this:

Me: "Howdy!" (I really wanted to say, "Where in the world did you come from?")

Young people: "How long are you going to be cutting the grass?"

To my way of thinking this was a very unusual beginning to a conversation. There was no polite small-talk and no mention whatsoever of the weather. But, my wife constantly reminds me to be polite so I simply answered their question.

Me: "I don't rightly know. I just got started. Why do you ask?"

Young people: "We're filming a movie across the creek and the sound of the mower is interfering with production. We can't just stop filming and wait until you finish. It will cost us too much money!"

This conversation was becoming more incredulous by the second. My only options were to take their word for it or call them both a big, fat liar.

Me: "Are you asking me to stop cutting my grass?"

Young people: "Yes!!"

The gist of the situation was they were indeed filming a movie across the creek from our house. They had been given permission by the owner to use his hunting lodge and the several hundred acres surrounding it for the purpose of filming what I can only surmise was a very low budget movie. Since they were asking a favor of me, I felt a few more questions were in order. It seems that in the movie they were filming, two young women were fleeing a very bad man in a remote and densely wooded area far from civilization. Maybe it was a re-make of the hit movie, Deliverance, with a new twist. The crew and actors had ridden four-wheelers from the hunting lodge and had no idea there was a house in the woods on the other side of the creek. According to the young fellow, who identified himself as the director and the young woman as his assistant, they had spent hours setting up the critical scene and had begun filming when the sound of my twenty-horse Cub Cadet had brought production to a screeching halt. It would have been time well spent if they had taken an additional twenty minutes to scout the area for people who reside in the woods. However, that was a moot issue at the time. It is indeed quite possible that the sound of a motor in the background would dispel any notion of being totally isolated in the woods. We do not go to the movies very often, but I could guess this scenario would have played havoc with the script. I agreed to delay my mowing for several hours and they turned and traipsed off toward the creek without even a simple thank-you. This answered my initial question of how they got in my yard: they had walked across the creek bottom. Before they disappeared down the hill into the woods, I shouted what I considered to be very good advice, "Keep an eye out for the ticks, copperheads, and cottonmouths!" I knew it was far too late to warn them about poison ivy. They would find out soon enough. The woman stopped momentarily, turned and looked at me in a very quizzical manner as if to say, "What are you talking about?" However, she was only the assistant and duty beckoned as she hesitantly followed her boss into the underbrush.

They left so abruptly I was not able to give advice on how southerners typically check for the presence of this trio of most unwelcome residents. A copperhead or cottonmouth is highly capable of announcing itself almost immediately and requires no expertise in determining if one is nearby. The close proximity of either of these critters can make a day turn out extremely bad. However, a tick is a totally different critter and requires a uniquely different method of detection. Normally, we remove all of our clothes, raise our arms above our head and dance around while a trusted companion of the opposite gender carefully scrutinizes for any sign of a tick. While this may seem odd to some folks, those of us who live in areas where ticks are known to reside realize the necessity of following sound professional advice. Some have suggested that music be added to this strictly medical procedure in an attempt to make it even more enjoyable.

A break in my story on grass cutting is necessary at this point in order for me to pontificate on one of the many ills of society. These thoughts frequently pop into my head at odd intervals, and my therapist has advised me to go ahead and get if off my chest, so to speak. The society that we live in today insists every activity must be structured so that it is enjoyable. For example, some obviously misguided people today insist that learning is fun and the classroom should be made more enjoyable for students. Fun in the classroom perverts the process as much as music perverts the intent of the southern tick dance. Most veteran educators will attest to the fact that once something becomes fun it is no longer educational. These stressed and wearied professionals continue to sit through extremely painful faculty meetings and pretend to listen while an administrator drones on and on about the exciting and innovative teaching techniques recently gleaned from a ten day all expenses paid seminar in Hawaii. On the other hand, their former colleagues who mistakenly bought into the theory that learning could be fun are now full time residents of The Village in Florida and spend their days playing golf with celebrities. Luckily, someone was wise enough to include a PTSD clause into their teaching contract which allowed early retirement when these misguided souls realized learning is generally difficult, takes time, and is often impossible for those who do not want to learn in the first place. They were so crestfallen by this revelation that early retirement was their only option.

Be that as it may, I feel obligated to return the conversation to the strange account of my encounter with the two movie makers in my front yard. It was extremely unfortunate that my unannounced visitors didn't linger long enough to take advantage of my sage advice, but they probably would have enjoyed that southern tradition so much they would never have gone back to California. Unfortunately, this happens to a lot of people who visit the South: they won't go back home. This curious and contagious phenomenon has now inflicted the Canadian geese which frequent our ponds. They apparently see no reason to follow centuries of tradition and return to their home in the far North. If I had to guess, they would have to use a compass to locate north. They like it here and simply refuse to leave.

Act two of this strange saga began immediately when I entered the kitchen where my wife was standing at the sink and looking at me in a quizzical manner. This conversation went something like this:

Wife: "I thought you were going to cut the grass."

Me: "I had to quit."

Wife: "Why?"

Me: "Some people from California are filming a movie across the creek, and the sound of the lawnmower is creating a real problem. They asked me to stop."

Wife: "Seriously, is something wrong?"

Me: "There is nothing wrong."

Wife: "Are you sick?"

Me: "No, I am not sick."

Wife: "Don't lie to me!"

Me: "I'm not lying!"

Wife: "I'm calling the doctor!"

Me: "I won't go!"

Wife: "If you don't want to cut the grass, just tell me."

Me: "I'll finish it later. I'm going to go to the shop and kill some rats!"

Anyway, those readers who have been married a long time understand the back story behind the conversation and the remainder can just sort of scratch their head and wonder how people stay married past the honeymoon.

My credibility was not only challenged by my wife, but the crowd I eat breakfast with every Friday morning was equally suspicious. We gather at a little café across the road from the cotton gin, and the clientele consists of farmers, fishermen, hunters, and other assorted liars and ne'er-do-wells. In other words, this is a hardcore group of men who have been known to exaggerate and never let the truth stand in the way of a good story. Normally, there are several conversations occurring simultaneously around the table, but everything got real quiet as they began to hear snippets of my incredible tale. There seemed to be an unusual amount of smirking and head shaking and their disbelief was all too obvious. I must confess I left breakfast that morning with my ears burning.

Word of my declining mental state traveled rapidly via the grapevine from the café to our church where I soon found my name on the prayer list. Naturally, my wife was curious as to why the church was praying for me. My reply was that I can use all the prayers I can get, and that is the truth if I ever told it. Skepticism ran rampant for several weeks at home and at the café until an article in the local newspaper confirmed my account. There was indeed a movie being filmed in the area by a group out of the state of California, and the story was not a product of my imagination. The article described in detail how the owner of the hunting club had offered the use of his land after a friend told him they were looking for a remote area in which to film the outdoor scenes. To my way of thinking, it wasn't remote enough. There was no mention made of snake bites or severe cases of poison oak.

Complete and total vindication is a wonderful thing! Vindication is a far better word to use and sounds much more refined than gloating. The yokels at the café were forced to eat crow as I waved a copy of the newspaper article in their faces. Eventually, the three words which have been the fuel to launch most marriages since cavemen began scribbling on walls of their cave are replaced by the four words which sustain these long-term unions: "I told you so." The newspaper article stayed attached to our refrigerator door until it mysteriously disappeared several weeks later. My only regret about the whole incident was in not demanding a bit role in the movie in return for my generous gesture to stop cutting grass. Surely, the charming neighbor on the Cub Cadet will at least be mentioned in the credits at the end of the movie. This could have been the day a star was born, but it was not to be.

One of the talents most people have is the ability to complain about most anything. We have perfected the art of whining, groaning, moaning, grousing, bellyaching, sniping, faultfinding, squawking, lamenting, whimpering, wailing, and being peeved at most anything and anybody depending on the circumstance. I do not exempt myself from any of the above descriptors. As a matter of fact, I enjoy participating in most of them. The absolute truth of the matter is that I have been richly blessed, because I am still healthy enough to cut my own yard. I know so many people who would love to have the strength to get out of the house and cut grass just one more time. But it goes much further than doing something mundane like using a lawnmower. God has blessed me greatly by the fact that I am still able to get out of bed every day and make plans for the day, whether that involves working in my shop, going to church, or visiting friends. What a wonderful blessing!!!!!

******

Oregon
Civilian
Conservation
Corp
←

Florence
Alabama →

Jackie Hastings

Go Take a Walk

A lot can be gained by just lying in the grass and gazing at the sky. As a boy, this was a favorite pastime of mine, although frequent interruptions had to be endured to respond to the demands of parents to do some chore they considered much more worthwhile. One can see many wonderful sights and an active imagination can create animals and people out of passing clouds. At times they are driven by a fierce wind and their shape changes constantly. Other times they just float lazily along like a leaf in a slow moving stream. Watching the flight of birds as they pass overhead can be entertaining as well as educational. I have read that Wilbur and Orville Wright studied how birds fly as they pondered how to get man off the ground and into the air. They observed how birds use air currents to soar along without using an ounce of muscle. It was then that they decided if man was to ever fly it would be by using his head and not his limited strength. They surmised that for a machine to stay in the air it would have to be able to move up and down and from side to side by using feathers and wing movements to develop lift. As I said, a lot can be gained by just lying on your back and staring into the sky.

As a boy I often lay in the grass and watched the birds soaring and flitting around over my head and wondered how it would be to actually fly. It has been a genuine blessing in my life that the world around me at that time didn't think that kind of activity rather odd. Any kid today who attempted to just look up and take the time to actually see the sky would get a close up view of their helicopter parents hovering directly overhead, directing them to their next practice, party, or recital. Mankind has labored for many years to produce leisure time just to observe and wonder at what is around us but, amazingly, there seems to be less of it today than at any other time in my own life. Kids growing up today have a lot more than we did but, in a very important sense, they have a lot less.

The occasional airplane overhead would get my mind to thinking about how it would be to actually go someplace else and see what the world was like in other places. My thoughts would drift to the question of where did it come from and, conversely, where is it going? Of course, it could have come from the local airport located across the river from my home-town and would return there very soon. Sometimes, generally on Sunday afternoons, my dad would take us to the airport just to watch the small planes take off and land. He would park in the grass close to the fence, and we would just sit on the hood of the car and watch. The airport was very small and very informal and other fathers apparently had the same idea as my dad. An easy and correct conclusion would be that recreational activities for families were very limited in those days, especially those that were free. Nowadays, folks loitering near an airport fence would be cuffed and interrogated by federal anti-terrorism authorities. After the questioning concluded, the unfortunate yokels would be placed on the No-Fly list. In our family, that would not have been a big problem because none of us ever thought we would have the opportunity to fly anyway.

There weren't many opportunities, actually no opportunities at all, for a kid in our community during the 1950s to take wings and fly, so it was simply speculation as to what it would be like.

Ignoring the time I fell out of my tree house and broke my arm, the next closest I came to flying as a boy was to stand on our very high back steps with a towel tied around my neck and leap to the ground, hoping to soar around the neighborhood like my hero, Superman. Unfortunately, the transformation never occurred and the Law of Gravity once again won out over a young boy's fantasy. The laws of physics make it much easier to leap to the ground from any height when you are ten years old and weigh maybe fifty pounds. This formula changes drastically when pounds and years are added, and the idea of leaping any-where vanishes completely from the thought process.

At our house we didn't get much encouragement to go zooming through the wild blue wonder from our daddy. The airport fence was as close as Daddy ever got to actually flying. It seems he had a morbid fear of flight and would not entertain the idea of ever leaving the ground. As a child he witnessed a very discouraging sight at one of the barnstorming events common in the early 1900s, where pilots toured the country in small planes. They were generally former WWI pilots stuck in a country now at peace with the world with no prospects for a job utilizing their flying skills. Airlines were a thing of the future. Thus, they were reduced to entertaining local bump-kins by aerial acrobatics and making a few bucks by taking the few brave souls with a couple of dollars for a spin around the skies of the neighborhood. Unfortunately, a not so smooth landing where the plane ended up on its back convinced my daddy-to-be that the friendly skies were not so friendly and that God never intended man to fly. He stuck by that philoso-phy for his entire eighty-seven years on planet earth. In spite of countless invitations from one of my brothers living out of town to visit and have his ticket paid for, he never once entered an airplane. He was a young boy when the Wright brothers lifted off from the sand dunes of Kitty Hawk, North Carolina, and he lived long enough to see an American set foot on the Moon. Yet, Daddy never changed his mind about flying. His policy was that he would be willing to fly anywhere as long as he could keep one foot on the ground. As a matter of fact, his fear of leaving solid ground would not even allow him to ride on an elevator. Many times as a kid I accompanied Daddy on errands in buildings several stories high with an elevator for easy access to the upper floors. The building that comes to mind at the moment was at the post office in downtown Florence. Unfortunately, my joy at riding on one of the elevators was always dashed by Daddy's refusal to take that risk, and we always ended up hoofing it up the stairs.

At that time of my life, elevators had an operator who sat on a small stool in the corner and made sure you made it to the correct floor. They also wore a uniform that would have made a general in a South American third-world country jealous. The necessity of having someone in an elevator to push the right button has always puzzled me. Apparently, Americans could not be trusted with the momentous decision of picking the floor they wished to visit by simply pushing the right number. This mentality makes me wonder how the West was ever won by such a timid and indecisive people, how Daniel Boone made his way back home after traveling thousands of miles alone in the wilderness, and how man managed to go to the Moon and safely back to planet Earth. Somehow, in spite of great danger, all these brave souls managed to find their way back home, but elevator travel must have been far more dangerous and required a guide.

Having said all this, it should be evident that our clan did not travel far from home, if at all. Today, we are able to travel further from our home in a matter of minutes than our grandparents did during their entire life if all the miles they traveled were compiled into one number. In fact, my wife and I have driven one hundred miles one way in order to shell out at least ten dollars for a bologna sandwich and eat it in what was once the grease pit of an old gas station. Then we turn around and drive one hundred miles back home so that we can brag to our friends about the wonderful experience. There is something dreadfully wrong with this picture.

Not too long ago, my wife and I felt extremely discombobulated because our family seemed to be spread out all over the northern hemisphere. Our daughter was in Seattle, our son and his wife were in Mexico, and our two grandsons were in Nashville attending a church camp. This might be routine for some folks, and that lifestyle doesn't merit a second thought in most places today. We couldn't wait until everybody got back "where they belonged."

But this was not always the case. Frequent travel outside of one's community was something some folks could not or would not do. Aside from going to town once or twice a month, people simply stayed at home. This was greatly influenced by the fact that they had no way to go anywhere. It was not unusual for families in our community to have absolutely no means of transportation except their own two feet. Today, walking is looked upon as a very good means of keeping fit and most of us should do more of it. Somewhere along the way, walking has since become recreational instead of a necessity. Consider the billions of dollars spent each year on walking shoes and apparel. The old brogans Grandpa used following a mule will not do in today's world. A good example of recreational walking would be the thousands of folks who walk the more than two thousand mile length of the Appalachian Trail each year. They endure incredible hardship during the course of this great adventure, putting their lives and jobs on hold. It becomes fun only after the walk is completed and the blisters are healed. A few hardy souls have made the trip many times. Apparently, walking can become very addictive.

However, my daddy, older brothers, and cousins told a story for many years which sort of carried the walking business to the extreme. There was a fellow in East Florence by the name of Basil who could have been the poster-boy for the "no way to get there" category. Due to the absence of a motorized vehicle, Basil was a notorious walker. Daddy frequently commented on the fact that Basil trotted around the community holding an imaginary steering wheel while making motor-like noises with his mouth.

This in itself is not unusual as I have frequently engaged in similar behavior and raced my friends around the community and actually shifted imaginary gears. We went so far as to stop at an imaginary gas station to fill up with imaginary gas. However, Basil carried it to extremes. Early in his life, he took out walking from Florence to Tuscaloosa to visit a sister. A map reveals that Tuscaloosa is pretty much due south of Florence, and today it is basically a north to south drive. Back then, the lack of adequate roads added a lot of east to west miles to the trip. It seems that somewhere along the road, a friend happened along and spotted Basil on his walk-a-bout. By this time, Basil was already well south of his home. By happenstance, the friend who encountered Basil along the road was a fellow from East Florence who knew him well.

The Good Samaritan was one of a passel of kids whose daddy ran a grocery store in East Florence. The business is still operating today, although it has transitioned from a small grocery store to a very popular deli serving breakfast and lunch to a large customer base. This establishment is famous for the extremely tasty fried sausages and burgers. Celebrities, both real and self-proclaimed, can be seen there on a regular basis. Someone suggested that simply driving past the place assures a person of a high cholesterol count, but there is no evidence to support that claim. Even if it is true, the food is definitely worth the risk. They open early and close early. It sure seems to be an improvement over selling milk, cigarettes, and bread on credit and hoping to be paid eventually.

Anyway, as the story was related to me by my cousin, Charles McDonald, the car passed the man walking along the lonely road without stopping. One can only surmise that someone surely must have said, "That man we just passed looks a lot like Basil." On a hunch, the car was turned around and low and behold, it was Basil! He was given a ride on into Tuscaloosa and dropped off with no mention as to how he would get back home. For a man with two good legs, this was not a problem. After his visit, Basil reversed directions and began walking north. He re-appeared in East Florence a short time later after apparently walking most of the way back home. There was no mention of him holding an imaginary steering wheel. This trip possibly inspired Basil to undertake a much greater adventure a few years later.

During the Great Depression of the 1930s, President Franklin Roosevelt created what was called the Civilian Conservation Corp, referred to most everywhere as the CCC. The purpose of this federal program was to put young, unemployed, unmarried men to work on federal projects all over the nation in an attempt to provide them meaningful work while actually improving roads, bridges, national parks and other such projects related to conservation and natural resources. These men were housed in camps all across the country and were provided meals, uniforms, housing, and medical care. Each camp was a complete community within itself. The pay was about $30.00 per month, a large portion of which each enrollee was required to send back home to help support families hurting in every way from the effects of the Great Depression.

The years between the beginning of the Great Depression and the beginning of World War II were very difficult on folks looking for a job. There were simply none to be found. Basil and some of my older brothers and uncles were very close in age and hung around together since there was no meaninful work available. Like many in the crowd, Basil's education had come to an end after elementary school. He was born and raised in the community we all knew as Railroad Hollow. This appropriately named community was simply a hollow in the center of Sweetwater with railroad tracks running alongside a small stream through the middle and a road on each side of the tracks and stream. Even as a young boy I had enough sense to know that the folks who lived in Railroad Hollow had hard times as close neighbors. This bit of knowledge came by way of personal experience, since I delivered papers in Railroad Hollow for several years and attended Brandon School with many kids who lived in the hollow. It was not easy for many of my customers to come up with the forty-five cents per week they owed me and the *Florence Times*.

According to the story as it was told for many years in my family, Basil applied for the CCC program, was found acceptable, and sent to Oregon. Apparently, the logic of the federal government was as inexplicable back then as it is now. Basil was sent about as far from his home in East Florence as possible. There were CCC camps all across the nation much closer to home, but for some reason President Roosevelt felt Basil could best serve his nation from the far Northwest corner of this great country. In spite of amenities far superior to what East Florence was able to offer at the time, Basil was not happy. He was one of those folks who didn't get out much, and his homesickness was too much for him to overcome. Not one to just sit and bemoan his situation, he took the bull by the horns, so to speak, and did what he had done all his life while living in East Florence: anytime he wanted to go somewhere, he took out walking, and this is exactly what he did. My dad always suspected that Basil had absolutely no idea how far he was from Sweetwater.

I have read that the bumblebee is actually too heavy to fly on its tiny wings, but, since the bumblebee doesn't know any better, it flies anyway. Basil was like a bumblebee in this respect.

He set out late one night and fully intended to make his way back to East Florence by any means possible, which included doing a whole lot of walking. He just didn't know any better. He probably chose the darkness of night to make his departure because he knew the folks in charge of the CCC camp would frown upon his plan and would probably have him locked up for his own safety. These camps were operated in a military-like manner as evidenced by the fact that reserve officers from the U. S. Army were placed in charge of each individual camp. In strictly military jargon Basil was going AWOL, even though he was not in the military at the time. They probably did search for Basil, but no one, even in their wildest dreams, would ever imagine he would be walking back to Alabama.

According to the story, Basil arrived back home in East Florence about five to six months after he was shipped out to the great Northwest. In Basil's words, it took "a while" to get back because of the lack of transportation. He walked until someone gave him a lift and hopped freight trains if they appeared to be headed in the right direction. The rest of the time he just spent walking. There is no doubt he had a lot of company on the road, because many American males were on the road seeking something better than the hopelessness they left behind. Regardless, he did make it back just in time to be drafted into the U. S. Army at the beginning of WWII. After basic training, Basil was sent to the South Pacific where he participated in the invasion of several of the islands in that theater of the war. It is highly possible that storming the beaches of South Pacific islands made a CCC camp in Oregon look a lot better. Ironically, after another stint in the military, Basil married a woman from Michigan and died while living in Detroit, a long way from his beloved boyhood home in East Florence.

Throughout history, massive upheavals such as natural disasters, world wars, and depressions have resulted in far-reaching changes to society as we know it. The same was true in the small community of East Florence. In the absence of the Great Depression and WW II, most of the males in our community would undoubtedly have stayed put and somehow scratched out an existence. However, the depression caused people to look for a greener pasture and the war, by necessity, took them out of a familiar environment and scattered them across the world. Someone once wrote a book about the difficulty of going home again, and it was no different for my brothers, uncles, cousins, and neighbors. Sure, some came back and picked up where they had left off. But many others, like Basil, saw the world from another angle, and the course of their lives took on an entirely different direction which led them far from East Florence. Families were established in places which had never even heard of the Sweetwater community. That is not to say it was bad, that is just the way it was.

It seems to me that our society is so mobile we tend to forget about how it was when a ride in a motorized vehicle of some kind was a luxury and not taken for granted. I was fortunate enough to inherit an old Studebaker from my brother Johnny when he left for the Air Force. I had just turned sixteen. However, most of my older brothers never owned a car until they left home and got married. While they were home at our daddy's house, they bummed rides or walked virtually everywhere they went. This was true for everyone in our little community. Many people walked to work, to church, to visit neighbors, to go to town, and even on what passed for dates. Maybe handing a teenager a walking stick would be a big improvement over automatically handing over a set of keys at the age of sixteen. It is hard for young folks today to imagine having to walk to visit your girlfriend. The humiliation would be unbearable. One good thing would be a corresponding drop in the number of out-of-wedlock children born to teenagers.

By the time my generation came along, it was a great day when we had the money to install an AM radio in the dash of whatever we were fortunate enough to drive to visit our girl-friends. Technology soon changed these old AM radios to the more modern FMs. A young guy had reached the absolute zenith of having arrived when he was able to purchase the latest in listening enjoyment: an eight-track player. We were able to listen to almost non-stop music without the annoying interruption of commercials. In rapid order came the tape cassette and the CD player. An MP3 player can now transfer literally thousands of songs to our eager ears without having to push a button or pick up the needle arm of a record player while we flipped the record over. Now, our cars come equipped with a television, a telephone, a fax machine, and the voice of some strange lady who always knows how to get to where we are going.

A funny story was told by a good friend about when he was a young man and "sparking" his girlfriend who lived several miles away. He did not have access to an automobile, so he had to stay at home or walk. A date back then might consist of visiting a girl at her home on Saturday and sitting in the swing on the front porch for a couple of hours before her father made it quite clear it was time to go home. There was no picking up the girl in a car and roaring off to the movie or a fast food place. There was also no coming home at all hours of the night. At our house we had to be in the house by ten o'clock, even when I was a senior in high school.

My friend tells of one particular night he walked to his girl's house and stayed very late. It was really dark on a cloudy night when he left her house and started out for home. He decided he could make better time by leaving the dirt road and cut across several pastures. The fact that it was dark did not bother him at all because this particular trip had been made so many times while hunting and palling around with his buddies. He knew that he could do it with his eyes closed. Anyone who has spent any time around cattle is familiar with the cattle paths in pastures. They follow the same meandering path back and forth while traveling to the barn and to the watering areas. They are creatures of habit and do not simply wander around aimlessly. My friend was following one of these paths by feel when he suddenly found himself astride what felt and sounded like a frightened cow.   The startled animal was stampeding through the pasture, bawling to beat the band. Scared out of his wits, he held on for dear life until the cow tired and finally came to a halt and he was able to slide to the ground. Grateful to be back on solid real estate, he attempted to piece together what had just happened. The only scenario which made any sense at all was that the cow had found a spot to lie down and rest and it happened to be right in the middle of the cow path headed in the general direction of his house. The cow's head was pointed toward him and neither my friend nor the cow knew of the other's presence until it was too late. My friend was just ambling happily along minding his own business when he walked astraddle the cow and her head passed between his legs. Suddenly, he found himself facing south on a northbound cow who was undoubtedly as surprised as my friend. The cow had already started getting to her feet, and bossy's rear end always comes up first when she tries to stand. As he fell forward, he was face down on her back and could only hold on for dear life. The one bright spot in the story was his good fortune in not walking astraddle of the farmer's big jersey bull which was also somewhere in the pasture. Courting a girl without a car could have been more hazardous than anyone imagined.

My brothers told numerous amusing stories about hauling our grandfather around the local community and to neighboring areas to visit his relatives. Our grandfather, or "Pa Mac" as we called him, lived with us for as long as most of us could remember. I never knew him to have a vehicle of his own and, to my knowledge, could not even drive. If he couldn't bum a ride from someone, he simply walked. To describe him as a homebody was putting it mildly but this was not uncommon at the time. Two of my brothers took him to North Carolina during the 1950s to visit our cousin Edgar. Naturally, they stopped to eat several meals along the way. One waitress at a roadside café informed my grandfather that his coffee, eggs, bacon, and toast would be seventy-five cents. He embarrassed my brothers by refusing to pay the full amount and loudly proclaimed to the entire café that it was worth only a quarter and that was all he would pay. After he stalked out they meekly paid the remainder of the tab and made note to warn future waitresses down the road they would pay whatever amount was owed after our grandfather paid what he thought it was worth. Back home, Pa talked for years about how bad the food was in North Carolina. Living and dying in the midst of family and friends who know you and are willing to be annoyed by your peculiar behavior is a special blessing from a loving God.

While I was too young to be included in the trip to North Carolina with my two brothers and Pa Mac, I did make a few trips to Corinth, Mississippi, mostly with my daddy or brothers to take our grandfather to visit our cousin Sinclair McDonald who lived near Corinth. Near Corinth is as close as I can get to describing where he lived because he and his family lived a long way from most anywhere. The word "rural" is a definite understatement. They had to walk toward town to go hunting. For some reason totally unknown to me, our cousin Sinclair was known as Sangster. I can understand why someone would not want to be called Sinclair, but Sangster is not a big improvement. Kids were not privy to much information back then so I never knew why our cousin was called Sangster. We made the trek to Corinth a couple of times a year and Sangster and his family reciprocated by visiting with us about that often. He had a rather large family with a lot of boys and most of them were about the same age as some of my older brothers.

In addition to the name, there was something else that puzzled me about the situation with our cousin. An old fellow we all called "Cousin John" lived with them and came to our house when they visited. I remember asking my daddy how we were related to John and he replied that John was not actually our cousin. It seems that during the Depression many people lost their homes and just sort of walked around the countryside hoping to find something better than whatever they had left behind. Many of the hoboes who frequented the railroads in our community were in this same category. Most were men who no longer had a place to call home and went from place to place looking for work and something to eat. According to my daddy, John just walked up to Sangster's house one day during the depths of the Depression, knocked on his door and offered to swap a day's work for a meal. He never left. John lived with our cousin from the early 1930s until he passed away sometime during the late 1950s. When John died, we took another trip to Corinth for his funeral. I never knew his last name or where he came from.

During the occasions we visited Sangster, his place was sort of frozen in time. In no way do I mean this in a derogatory sense, because that was just the way it was all over the South. There was no indoor plumbing, there were no screens on the doors or windows, and the farm animals were not always confined. The local fly population had a field day at Sangster's house. By necessity the windows were left open during warm weather. Air conditioning at that time was neither available nor affordable for most people in the Deep South. This made for much easier access for the flies and a mule who stuck his head in the window on one visit while we were eating lunch. This was an unusual occurrence for the visiting family but no one else seemed to think it was unusual. The mules were an essential part of the livelihood for his family, and our cousin worked alongside them almost daily.

Unfortunately, the absence of the mules played a role in the death of our cousin Sangster. He was killed in a tragic accident when I was a teenager. The transition had finally, and reluctantly, been made from mules to an old Ford tractor. This miracle of the Machine Age rolled over on him while traversing a hillside on his farm.

As often happens, families lose track of each other when the patriarchs pass away, and this is what happened. There is no doubt many of Sangster's descendants are still in the Corinth area, but the two branches of the family have lost touch with each other. The younger folks in both families are not aware of the existence of their cousins who live only a short distance across a state line. Today's roads are straighter, wider, and make traveling much faster, but the distance is much greater because what we once had in common has disappeared with time.

Being able to "get away" from the daily grind, if just for a little while, can be extremely therapeutic even if we don't know what therapeutic means. A quick trip to Chattanooga by an old fellow who made his way around our small community on a wagon pulled by a couple of mules opened up a whole new world for him and provided the gist for a story which still makes me laugh every time it is repeated. The fellow at the center of the story had never been anywhere much outside of the community of East Florence in which we lived. A friend had to go to Chattanooga for a quick trip to take care of some family business and invited him to go along for the ride. A passenger train left East Florence early in the morning on a daily basis and passed through Chattanooga on its way north. The trip took about three hours one way, and another train headed south could return travelers to Northwest Alabama by late in the evening. It made for a long day but at least you didn't have to walk.

The two travelers arrived safely and departed the northbound train at the downtown Chattanooga depot and quickly took care of the necessary business. They had a couple of hours to spare while awaiting the return trip, so they rubbernecked around the big city and took in a few sights. Deciding to eat a quick snack before returning to the depot to await their train ride back to Alabama, they entered a small café about a block from the train station. The old fellow being perpetually low on funds ordered only a cup of coffee. As waitresses world-wide are prone to do, she asked him if he wanted dessert with his coffee. Apparently seized by a sudden impulse to splurge, he said he believed he would have a piece of pie. When asked what kind of pie he had in mind, he replied with a response which lived on for years in his small community. He said, "sweet-tater aye goddy, what other kind er thar?" This simple statement by a simple man has made me and many others laugh for years, but it also tells a story in itself about survival in the South during the Great Depression. Easily grown staples such as the common sweet potato and the turnip saved many from starvation during that terrible time. Over the years, I have heard many people say, including my own daddy, that had it not been for "possum and sweet taters" many more people would have gone to bed hungry all over the South.

The popular music group, Alabama, almost encapsulated the history of the modern South and my family, in their song, "Song of the South." Some of the lyrics include:

Song, song of the South

Sweet potato pie and I shut my mouth.

Gone, gone with the wind

Ain't nobody looking back again.

Well, somebody told us that Wall Street fell, but we were so poor we couldn't tell.

Cotton was short and the weeds were tall

But Mr. Roosevelt's gonna save us all.

Momma got sick and Daddy got down.

The county got the farm and they moved to town.

Poppa got a job with the TVA

He bought a washing machine and then a Chevrolet.

Indeed, our family did lose our house during the Depression, but then, believe it or not, Daddy got a job with the TVA. He bought a very small frame house, a Silvertone radio from Sears, and a wringer washer which was kept on the back porch. Our dryer was kept in the back yard and operated solely on wind and solar power. It consisted of a thin wire stretched between two poles, and it would not work on rainy days. By the way, Daddy bought a used Plymouth in spite of the fact that our favorite person on television, Dinah Shore, told a national audience every week that Americans could, "See the USA in your Chevrolet." For some reason, Daddy never liked Chevrolets.

Many families have handed down stories of the hard times experienced during and after the Civil War, which devastated large portions of the South. It has been said, and rightly so, that the Great Depression was simply an extension of the hard times many southerners felt following the War Between the States. A story in my family handed down from that time concerns my great great-grandfather, a fellow by the name of Josiah Higgins. It seems that Josiah was highly peeved by the sight of Federal gunboats patrolling the Tennessee River near his hometown of Waterloo. This beautiful part of our state is located in the extreme northwest corner of Alabama, across the river from Mississippi and almost touching the state of Tennessee. It was, and is to this day, a very isolated and rugged part of the world. Josiah, along with other members of the little home guard he had organized, took it upon themselves to drive the gunboats away by firing a few shots at them from the hills surrounding the river. Maybe they were just reminding the Yankees which side they were on, but it is never a good idea to attack a heavily armed gunboat with a few muzzle loaders. Naturally, the invaders from the North were highly peeved as well. It is never a good idea to irritate someone who is better armed than yourself. It wasn't exactly the same as showing up at a gunfight with a knife but it was real close. The next morning the federal government moved three gunboats in and shelled the town of Waterloo. Eventually, Josiah was taken prisoner and hauled off to a Union prison somewhere up north, and he wound up in prison near St, Louis, Missouri. After the war ended, Josiah was released and left to his own devices to find his way back home. Possibly, as he walked all the way back to Waterloo, Josiah had plenty of time to ponder if he had made the right decision. Regardless, he lived the rest of his life with a mighty poor opinion of Yankees.

A good friend who grew up during the Great Depression laughingly told the story of a fellow lucky enough to have a job at the local saw mill as an "off-bearer." This person was charged with keeping the slabs moved away from the blade. Standing in the bull pen next to a large, sharp blade was a hard and dangerous job. Ironically, the slabs he stacked were often free firewood and kept many families warm during long, cold nights. In any event, he soon grew tired of the same old lunch his wife prepared for him every day. There is no doubt a lack of money greatly reduces our options in a lot of ways, and monotony is something all of us attempt to avoid. Be that as it may, he happened to notice a fellow worker who always grabbed his lunch bucket and ate by himself behind a stack of lumber in the yard away from the other mill hands. Convinced the other fellow had a good lunch and simply did not want to share it, he contrived to swap lunch buckets and eat the other fellow's meal for himself. So one day at the noon break, he rushed off and switched lunch pails with the other fellow. Eagerly anticipating something different from what he had been eating for weeks on end, he opened the lunch bucket and, to his utter dismay, found the meal he had so long envied was nothing but a hickory nut and a hammer.

What further evidence do we need that we should never covet anything belonging to our neighbor? Sometimes we have it made and just don't know it.

******

Jackie Hastings

Goats

During the course of my life, I have had a lot of experience with goats. In all of God's creation, there is nothing more appealing to the human eye than a baby goat, commonly called a "kid." Goats have many good qualities and a few not so good ones. Some goats are very gentle while some are bullies. Some are very aggressive while others are meek as baby kittens. In this respect, they are a lot like people. Goats make very good pets, although having a goat running through my house is not very appealing. Dog owners will tell you that sometimes a dog tends to grovel at the feet of people. On the other hand, cat owners do not really own a cat, they just let it live in their house and feed it. All the while, the cat thinks it is doing its owner a favor. A goat can be sort of an equal opportunity kind of pet. It will treat you as an equal and will never grovel or "take on airs" as my mother used to say.

One of the not so good qualities of a goat is that they tend to smell, particularly the males. This is another negative trait they share with humans. My very first encounter with a very rancid goat came when I traded a small Shetland pony for a goat, sight unseen. The bargain was sealed over the phone. The owner of the goat was a truck driver and was not often at home. Our deal required me to load the pony in the back of my old truck equipped with wooden sideboards and deliver it to the man's house where I would find the goat tethered to a tree in the yard. As a matter of fact, that was to be the indicator which told me I have arrived at the right house in an adjacent county. After steering me to the right road his next set of directions was something to the effect, "it will be the first house on the left with a goat tied to a tree in the front yard. You can't miss it." I was to leave the pony tied to the same rope.

Loading the pony was not a problem because I had a ramp for that very purpose. However, my problem was how to load the goat into my truck after allowing the pony to simply jump the short distance to the ground. Now, the goat could have easily jumped into my truck had he so desired because goats are quite nimble. They are also very stubborn. Hence, the term, "stubborn as a billy goat," means something to those familiar with goats. No amount of coaxing could persuade the goat to do my biding, so I took the goat by the horns, so to speak, and bodily lifted him into the truck bed. He did seem rather miffed at such a personal encounter with a total stranger but, I suspect, was willing to tolerate it to get away from being tied to a tree. It had rained at intervals during the day and the goat was wet. In addition, the critter had enough hair to make him resemble a small Musk Ox. To simply describe his smell as rancid would be the understatement of the year. Naturally, the smell immediately transferred to my clothes and to the inside of my truck cab. Upon arriving at home, the clothes were easily discarded and had to be burned. However, my skin had absorbed the smell by osmosis, and no amount of my faithful Old Spice soap-on-a-rope made any difference. In comparison, a skunk would have smelled like Midnight in Paris, or something like that. My wife suggested Comet cleaner applied with a wire brush, but it was a hopeless cause. The only cure would have been a skin transplant or just let it wear itself out. I chose the latter and my marriage barely survived.

The goat never really lost the bad smell, even when it was bone dry. In addition, there were several other bad qualities associated with this particular goat. He had an unnerving tendency to stand on the hill above our house and just stare at us when we ventured outside. It was as if his eyes were wide open with some sort of evil intent behind them. Some in the mental health profession might refer to his stare as a "psychotic stare." In horror movies this is recognizable because the whites of the eyes are always visible. The goat's stare was made even worse because his eyes were not white but yellow around the edges and sort of red in the middle. In addition, he possessed a set of horns which would have made a Texas longhorn bull jealous. Occasionally, the goat was able to somehow get his head lodged inside a section of the net wire used on the pasture fence. Once this happened, it was impossible for him to free himself because of the horns. It was kind of like pulling an imbedded fishhook out of your skin. When he realized he was trapped in the fence he began bleating. The decibel level exceeded what the government considered to be safe for human ears. This, combined with the fact that the prevailing wind brought his disgusting smell to the house, made him a prime contender to be sold or traded. No wonder his previous owner was so anxious to get rid of him. We finally had to give him away with one condition: his new owner was responsible for transporting him to his new home. There was no way I was going to try and load that goat again.

All the goats we owned were bought for the purpose of keeping the weeds and brush under control. They do an excellent job, but in the process will consume flowers, shrubs, and the entire garden unless contained inside a fence. Over the years we have owned everything from common brush goats to registered Nubians and Boers to what we called "fainting" or "nervous" goats.

Most folks ridicule the notion of a goat just passing out when alarmed, but it is true. My credibility has been constantly questioned by a never-ending train of unbelievers who scoff at my fainting goat stories. Realizing my good name was at stake, it became incumbent upon me to do the proper research on the topic. According to the experts, a myotonic goat, otherwise known as a fainting goat, is a domestic goat whose muscles freeze for roughly ten seconds when the goat feels panic. This is a painless condition, although the goat normally collapses on its side for the duration of the panic attack.

The condition is hereditary and is called myotonia congenita. Now that the facts have been straightened out, my story about goats will continue.

Our children and their equally mischievous friends often entertained themselves for hours by stalking our herd of "fainting" goats. Some child-raising experts might suggest children who enjoy such activities also suffer from a hereditary disorder as well, but that is only speculation. Besides, it kept them out of the house for long periods of time. The little urchins became as stealthy as a band of Apaches waylaying a wagon train. Their singular purpose was to intentionally frighten the goats and watch gleefully as most of the herd fell to the ground as stiff as a two-by-four. The younger members of the herd are more likely to collapse. Some of the older goats have learned to lean on a nearby object and stand stiff-legged until they regain the use of their legs. In the meantime, they are totally incapacitated. Pestering the goat herd and swinging on grape-vines on the hillside overlooking the creek helped keep our children from feeling deprived. The creative ways they conjured up to entertain themselves went unappreciated by the goats. Obviously, in addition to the afore-mentioned children, the fainting goats are also vulnerable to predators.

A fellow in our community once raised a male fainting goat on a bottle after the nanny-goat died shortly after giving birth. Raising a goat on a bottle can be a great experience for the entire family but the goat can become quite annoying and demanding once it becomes mature. My friend's goat quickly became a part of the family and was given full run of the place, except inside the house. However, it did have a fondness for standing on the porch and watching television through the window. The goat developed an identity problem and did not come to grips with the fact he was a goat. It often ran around with my friend's pack of beagle hounds when his human family was not around. There is a lesson here for parents when their children take to running around with unsavory friends.

Anyway, my friend was an avid rabbit hunter, and the goat was fond of accompanying him even while hunting. Eventually, the goat took to running with the dogs even when they were chasing rabbits. This was quite unique. Obviously, the goat contributed nothing to the chase because he was unable to bark or sniff out the rabbit. He just, as our British friends might say, enjoyed "running with the hounds." On one particularly sad day, the hunt carried the pack of dogs out of the creek bottom and across the only major highway in the vicinity. Unfortunately, as the fainting goat was crossing the road, a log truck came around the curve at a high rate of speed. All in all, this type situation was a disaster in the making, especially for any creature with the sensitive nervous system of a fainting goat. As one might expect, it did not turn out well. The driver set down on his rather loud horn when he saw the dogs and goat in the middle of the road. The dogs were able to scurry off to the side but the poor fainting goat became a victim of his peculiar central nervous system. The loud noise from the rapidly approaching truck caused him to faint and, unfortunately, a fully-loaded log truck cannot stop on a dime.

Upon his demise, the legend of the rabbit-hunting goat grew far out of proportion. However, it remains a topic of conversation in certain circles in our community to this very day. The unbelievers are still in the majority, and maybe it is one of those things which have to be seen to believe.

******

Jackie Hastings

Helping my Dad

My situation was precarious at best. Dad was at the wheel of his Massey Ferguson tractor with his bush hog attached to the rear, which turned it into sort of a platform. Unfortunately, I was sitting on the bush hog with a five-gallon bucket of yellow delicious apples we had just picked from one of his trees at the back of his pasture. Trudging along behind the tractor and eating the apples out of my hand was Dad's extremely large Charolais bull which went by the name of "Big Pete." Actually, the bull didn't answer to any name, but Pete was the one we used around mixed company. My predicament started out bad and was getting progressively worse by the apple. The bucket was almost empty and the barn was not even in sight.

Big Pete was not one to take "no" for an answer. It did not take much for Pete to get aggravated real fast. The big white bull topped the scales at about two thousand pounds, which is a ton of bull in anybody's book. Being big isn't necessarily bad, but being big and extremely aggressive and practically living in your backyard is not a good combination. Pete had started out as a family pet but close proximity to people had robbed him of his fear and respect. In other words, he had turned rogue. It was not a good idea to get caught on foot anywhere close to Pete. It didn't take waving a red flag to get his attention, and once you got his attention, it was good to have a gate or tree nearby. Dad finally got the message the day Pete attacked the tractor, ripping the lights off and punching a hole in the sheet metal with a horn. My dad was a hard-headed man, but the fact he was driving the tractor when Pete attacked made quite an impression on him. Pete was big and mean but he was not too smart. The big bull had just committed a cardinal sin because the shiny red Massey-Ferguson was my daddy's pride and joy.

It was for this very reason that we were trying to lead him into the corral beside the barn. Daddy had sold him to a fellow and part of the deal was that he would come and haul him away, but we had to first get him into the barn. It was far too danger-ous to "herd" him on foot, so we thought the apples would be sort of like the proverbial carrot on a stick. I could hear Daddy laughing when I turned from my perch on the bush hog, which was about two feet from Pete's massive head and said, "Daddy, you better drive faster, we're about out of apples." My dad's per-severance paid off once more, and Pete's love for apples eventu-ally proved to be his undoing. He was also dealing with a fellow who never gave up and tried to instill that type character in all his children. At the end of the day, Dad and I had the pleasure of watching and waving as the big bull made like Elvis and "left the building."

Memories of the times spent with my dad are among the best of my entire life. I was his go-fer on hundreds of occasions from the time I was just a little boy until he passed away in the nursing home at the age of eighty-seven. For those who don't know, go-fer is a term currently used to describe a person, gen-erally a child, who is learning to do tasks and is sent to fetch items. Working with my dad, I became so good at fetching he should have named me "Lassie."

Daddy was a jack-of-all-trades, but he worked primarily as a carpenter. He learned the wood-working trade from his father, Jesse William McDonald, who was also a carpenter and cabinetmaker. It is common knowledge that carpenters are constantly in need of someone to go fetch his saw, bring him a handful of nails, fetch his level, bring him a drink of water, hold a piece of wood, fetch his brace-and-bit, or any one of dozens of other chores required to finish a project. When I was old enough to get my driver's license, Daddy got me a job through the local carpenters' union working as a carpenter's helper. At that time, there really was a job with that name. Not an apprentice, but a helper. In other words, I was being paid to do something that I had already been doing for free. This was a job I had trained for all my life, and the learning curve was very short.

In my eyes my dad could do anything, build anything, and fix anything that was broken. Apparently, many others felt the same way. His reputation had spread far and wide as he was called upon by all manner of family, friends, and simple acquaintances to repair something or build something new at their home or business. As my older brothers were gradually eliminated from consideration by marriage or the military, the job of helping Dad became mine by default. But, unlike many kids, I loved every minute of it. Carpentry was not the only thing Dad was good at. He was a pretty fair hand as a plumber, roofer, sheet metal worker, brick mason, electrician, and gadget fixer. With my dad as my guide, the do-it-yourself bug soon affected me and has been passed successfully on to my son and daughter.

My Dad was 75 years old when this picture was taken. The pine tree was standing in the way of a building project and he decided it must go. Cutting the tree at ground level would have likely caused it to crash onto his house. So, he did what any 75 year old would do: he climbed into the very top of the fifty-foot tree and cut it off one section at a time as he climbed back down. He failed to understand why his children thought it was a bad idea.

My dad was not prone to go out and buy stuff. Nor was he likely to hire somebody to do something he could obviously do for himself. It seemed to run counter to his very nature. This was proven time after time during all the years I knew him. One day I showed up at his house only to find him about forty feet up a large pine tree trimming limbs. He was about eighty years old at the time, but could not understand why I was alarmed. Some might say he was tight-fisted with his money as a result of his Scottish heritage, but that was not the case at all. He never had any money to be tight-fisted with and adjusted his situation accordingly.

William Ervin McDonald was my father. He was born November 10, 1903, and died November 11, 1990, one day beyond his eighty-seventh birthday. He rests now beside our mother, Pauline, in the cemetery behind Pleasant Hill United Methodist Church in the Central community of Lauderdale County. What began as the lonely burial site for our mother now contains the graves of both of my parents, three brothers, a nephew, one aunt, and one uncle.

Daddy was a graduate of the school of hard knocks if there ever was one. He should have been the valedictorian of the class. If there was ever an Easy Street in his life, he never lived there. He only drove past it on his way to work. His mother died when he was about five years old, about six months after giving birth to a third son named Chalmus. My Dad was the oldest, my uncle Alphonse was the second son, and Chalmus was the third child. Chalmus died shortly after his second birthday, leaving my grandfather with two sons to raise without a mother, since he never re-married. Relatives and friends helped him solve the problem by providing a home for his children. My uncle Alphonse was taken in by the Butler family and my daddy went to live with his mother's sister, Mary Frances Redding Rickard. She quickly became the most important person in his young life, and he always referred to her as "Aunt Bummie." Her children, Hunter, Homer, Frank, and Alta Belle became his instant family. It took me many years to realize how important they were to him.

When we were kids, Daddy would take us to the old Sears store on Tennessee Street around Christmas and let us wander wide-eyed through the toy department. For many years, they had a marvelous display of a model train on a large platform with little towns, bridges, rivers, tunnels, forest, cars. In other words, everything that caused a train-loving boy to feel the beginnings of lust in his heart. If Daddy had other things to do, he just left me drooling beside the display. I would have sold my birthright for a train but it was not to be. He had an entirely different policy. If I told him I needed a bow and arrow because the blood of Geronimo or Cochise was temporarily flowing in my young veins, he had the answer. Soon, one night, after a long day at work, we would go out to his shop and together we would construct a bow that would have made Hiawatha happy. Out of a rusty piece of steel he made me a knife that rivaled the one that made Jim Bowie famous. Together, we made a marvelous home-plate out of a thick piece of white rubber which was the envy of the boys in the neighborhood and became a mainstay at all the sandlot baseball games in the community. On his lathe, he turned a baseball bat out of a piece of willow that would swat a ball so far it was surely banned by the big leagues. It was a matter of pride to me that he considered me trustworthy enough to have access to his workshop and the tools inside. Woe unto me if I failed to return a tool to its proper place. If I ever heard him say, "Boy, where's my handsaw?" I knew a stern lecture was on the way.

Thankfully, my memories of my father do not consist of all the stuff he bought me. If that had been the case, my memories of him would be very brief and shallow. It was much later in my life that I realized the greatest gift my daddy gave me was the time we spent together. As an adult, it came as quite a shock to me to learn that all daddies didn't wrestle with their kids on the living room floor, play baseball in the back yard, and go deep into the woods on a cold winter day and drag home a sorry-looking Christmas tree. He did his very best to teach all his kids how to survive in a world that had not been very kind to him.

My dad's formal education ended in the sixth grade. That was not unusual at all at the time because most kids had to work to help their family survive. Dad helped his own father and learned the carpenter's trade from him. He followed my grandfather across the community and to other towns and states doing various jobs. They lived together in a railroad box car near Sweetwater, Texas helping harvest the cotton crop one year. It was in Texas he saw his very first jackrabbit. After listening to him tell about the critter's size and speed, I was real glad they lived in Texas and not in Alabama. He told me of being inside a boiler at the Cherry Cotton Mill, cleaning the scale from the walls for fifty cents a day during the Great Depression. Why, I asked? His answer was very simple: to buy food for his family. This was the life he lived until he was old enough to go out on his own.

Many times as we drove through East Florence, he pointed out the site of the old Acme Lumber Company where he had his first real job. As I recall, it was located behind the old foundry in East Florence down toward the canal. He helped build wooden coffins for the victims of the deadly world-wide flu epidemic of 1918. Later, he worked as a café cook, and this was where he undoubtedly developed his love for cooking. There is no doubt my wife was extremely disappointed to learn this was one skill her husband did not inherit from his father. Dad also worked as a painter, installed gas tanks for the Standard Oil Company, served a stint as a photographer's assistant, drove a bus every day from Florence to Russellville and frequently took one of his boys along just for the ride. During the hard times of his life, he was the first in line for any job which would let him earn a dime. As an adult he worked on the old Riverton Lock in Colbert County during the 1920s. He was helping build the original St. James Methodist Church on Sweetwater Avenue in East Florence when he left for Massachusetts to work on the Cape Cod Canal system. He enthralled his kids with the story of watching a huge whale swim beneath him while he was working high atop a bridge near Boston. Many times he told me he came close to freezing and didn't understand how people could live in such a cold, windy place.

My father was one of the first to be employed by the Tennessee Valley Authority in November, 1933. He eventually became the head carpenter foreman for the National Fertilizer Research and Development Center and worked at that job until he retired in the late 1960s. Working at TVA was a godsend for my daddy because he was just beginning to emerge from one of the darkest periods of his life, and there had been many from which to choose. As a result, my parents with their three old-est sons, along with my grandfather, were forced to live in two tents for two years. With no work to support his family, my dad and oldest brothers peddled fire wood from door to door in an effort to put together enough money for their next meal. In an interview a few years before he died, my brother Bill described the situation as he remembered it:

My dad and mother were renting a house and it took every-thing they had-the Depression did-even a lot of Mother's furniture. We literally moved out of the house into two tents. Two tents-one of them was a living area and sleeping area, the other was a kitchen which was curtained off so that my Grandfather McDonald had a little privacy in his room. He always lived with us.

In order to eat, my dad got permission from the people who owned what we called the Woodland, which is now Edgemont sub-division in Florence. The forest had been cut, leaving the stumps pretty high. My dad got permission from those people that owned the land to cut those stumps down to the ground level. We cut those stumps with a crosscut saw and hauled them in with a two-wheeled cart that he made. He would pull the cart and I would get behind and push it.

We would get down to our home: which was literally two tents. We stacked our stumps up. When we could, we split them up and managed to sell them around Florence, pushing the cart and selling stove wood, we called it. Sometimes we would swap the stove wood for butter and eggs and milk.

Generally speaking, we didn't go hungry. But we didn't eat fancy either. We had a rough time. I remember the winter of 1932. It was an extremely cold winter. We didn't have shoes to wear. Mother kept me home from school.

The Depression had a great impact on Mother. She had been reared with better things than we. She was accustomed to having a better lifestyle than what she found after she married Daddy and the Depression hit. She was always recollecting and talking about those days. She would always tell me, "Now don't ever tell people how poor we were." That was an embarrassment to her.

Literally pecking out an existence under conditions he described as, "the wolf was constantly at the door," made him determined to move his family to the country where they could more easily provide for themselves during hard times.

All of W. E. McDonald's children could go on and on reciting things we remember about him and what he taught us. But, once more, let me refer back to something my brother Bill wrote about our dad. He put it best many years ago when he penned a piece about our father as we gathered to celebrate Father's Day. The piece is entitled, *Twisted Nails and Long Ago*. It is now framed and hangs on the wall in our home. In its entirety, it reads:

Dad is very much alive and doing well, thank you. His step is sure, and his gait is that of a man many years younger.

When I think on these things I'm reminded of not so long ago watching him from my bed at the Seale Harris Clinic in Birmingham. This took my mind off of my own problems as he jogged across the mountain side....and I counted the times he passed my window.

Father's Day is a well-deserved honor. We get a big kick, though, in thinking about what it would take for any one of his grown children to catch up with this fellow long enough to present our tribute. By his own account he is much too busy for things like that.

But, all of us have a lot to say. It's really an adventure to think back across all the years we've had with Dad. We, no doubt, could write a book about the things he stood for, and the lessons he gave. I'm convinced now that he was making sure that we'd be prepared for the things in life he suspected would someday come our way.

One simple, yet important, strategy was the way he taught us to drive a nail. It mattered not whether we were hammering on the back side of the barn, or out front where everybody could see. None of his boys would keep driving a twisted or bent nail. Each mistake was not to be ignored, but carefully extracted, and replaced with a better one that we'd never be ashamed for anyone later to find.

There are occasions even now when it's tempting to make do, or patch up, or even cover over, a mistake that surely no one else will catch or notice. It is times like these that I recall the nail and those other carefully constructed lessons learned long ago. Dad would say that if it's worth doing at all it's worth doing right...and...you can tell a good carpenter by the way he drives his nails...and...that a man would never be sorry that he corrected an error, no matter how small.

I'm thinking tonight of the role that Daddies play in the rearing of children. No gift for him, I'm sure would mean half as much...if somehow we could find a way to really say "thank you" on this special Father's Day.

My brother's recollection of how our dad taught his sons to drive a nail brought to mind another story about nails. During the late 1950s and early 1960s, my dad's dream of moving to the country was finally coming true. We were building our house on a few acres he had purchased west of Florence in the Central community. The house was in the dry and Daddy had contracted with a fellow he worked with at TVA to stub in all the plumbing. Many years later this fellow told me that normally when he was working a job and needed a nail, all he had to do was look down and pick up a bent nail which had been discarded by the builders. Not so at our house he said. He was amazed that he could not find a single nail on the floor in the whole house. This was highly unusual around a house under construction. The explanation was quite simple. Every time a nail was bent it had to be straightened and used. A nail dropped to the floor had to be picked up. Old habits die hard!

Several years ago, one of my nephews came to my house and, for a reason that now escapes me, we went out back to my work shop. As soon as he walked in the door, he said, "Uncle Tommy, your workshop looks exactly like I remember Daddy Ervin's (the name given him by his grandchildren) looked when I was a little boy." I had never thought about it, but sure enough, it did. There was barely enough room to walk. Tools were hanging in every available space, pieces of wood were leaning against the walls, unfinished projects were stacked on work benches, the smell of cedar wood shavings on the floor, and a faint whiff of smoke from the fire burning in my wood stove. He asked if I had purposely made it look like my dad's.

No, it just worked out that way for some reason.

******

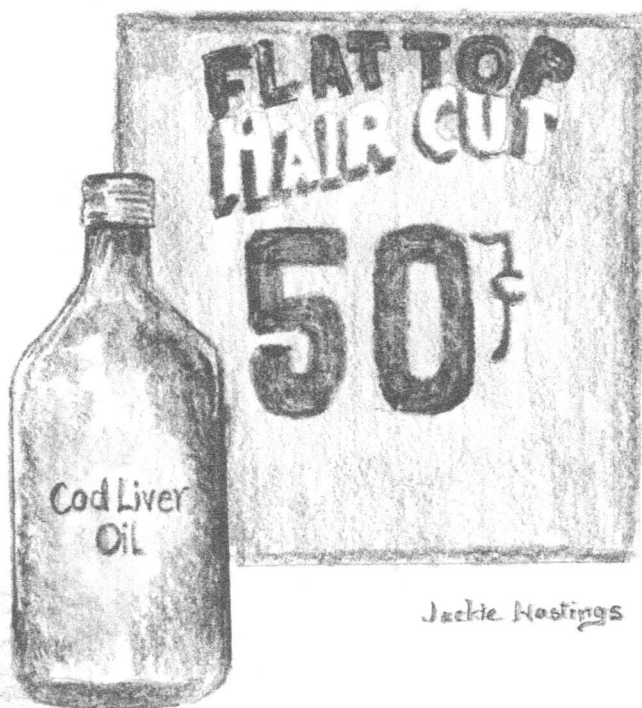

FLATTOP
HAIR CUT
50¢

Cod Liver
Oil

Jackie Hastings

How Did We Survive?

Apparently, it is the inherent right of the older generation to annoy the younger folks with a never-ending litany of stories about how things were different and more difficult and somehow better when they were growing up. It was that way when I was a kid, and this millennial generation, as it is often referred to by the media for some strange reason, should have to suffer just as generations before suffered. It has been said that this current crop somehow feel they are entitled, but I have no idea what goes through anybody's mind, not even my own as of late. Our society at times seems to be fixated on feelings and what others are thinking, but what do I know? Be that as it may, this current generation may truly be entitled to the best jobs, cars, homes, and technological gadgets money can buy, but they are definitely not entitled to an exemption from the misery of listening to their elders expound on life in the dark ages. The old saying that misery loves company is probably appropriate for this situation. The fact that most of us had to walk five miles uphill to school in the snow has been well documented and should need no further elaboration. A side note here might be to add that we also had to carry our lunch in an old molasses bucket which generally consisted of nothing more than a cold slab of cornbread as an entrée with a mayonnaise sandwich for dessert. It is not true we had to fight dinosaurs and sabre-tooth tigers along the way. Our grandchildren instigated that particular rumor. How did we survive?

When our children were small they had the usual childhood illnesses, scrapes, and bruises. They also had the benefit of a mother with a driver's license and a vehicle to whisk them to the doctor at a moment's notice. They were so accustomed to visiting the doctor that they began crying long before they reached his office. Each had a built in GPS which kicked in when they came in close proximity, and the tears began to flow. This took place so frequently that I came to resent the fact that my children's doctor drove around town in a Cadillac convertible while I was struggling along in a Ford Falcon with a transmission that constantly popped out of third gear. This old car could be parked in a high crime area with the window down and the motor running without any fear of it being stolen. The only good thing about driving a Falcon was that getting a ticket for excessive speed was as rare as finding teeth in a rooster.

On that topic, most young folks today have no concept of a transmission in the first place. They grew up driving vehicles which only required pressing the accelerator to achieve forward motion. Manually shifting from gear to gear in order to make the vehicle move forward, while simultaneously coordinating the clutch with a shift lever on the steering column, requires more focus than can be mustered by brains and reflexes which have become mushy from excessive texting. Just for old time's sake, I would love to observe one more time a frustrated parent in the passenger seat and a not-so-cool teenager behind the wheel in a car in the throes of the herky-jerky take-off characteristic of a new driver who had not yet coordinated the release of the clutch with pressure on the gas pedal. This scenario could be spotted a mile away, and the goofy teenager always blamed the parent.

In my Neanderthal opinion, it would be a much safer world if all sixteen year olds had to master a manual transmission before being allowed on the road. This one requirement would render them virtually immobile until they were at least twenty years old, and this would be very good for our society. In fact, our children had to meet this very requirement because they had no other option. We owned, in partnership with the bank, a car and a truck and both had manual transmissions. In addition, we would not allow our children to go for their driver's test until they proved they could stop at the top of a hill, shift into low gear, and then move forward without rolling backward down the hill. This required nerves of steel on the part of my wife and me, because this particular skill does not come naturally and demands a great deal of practice. Rolling backward down a steep hill with a panicked teenager behind the wheel is not recommended and can quickly ruin a pleasant drive through the back roads. For this very reason we always kept a spray can of Valium on hand in order to quickly calm frayed nerves.

A friend tells a similar story of her father requiring all his children to drive in reverse across a narrow, one-lane, wooden bridge high above Cypress Creek in our rural community. Driving in reverse is definitely a good practice for young folks, but, in my humble opinion, the reverse gear should be removed from the vehicles of all people over the age of sixty. At this age, most of us cannot see behind us, thereby rendering the use of the rear view mirror a total waste of time. Instead, most just back up and know they have gone far enough when they hear metal crunching. Any means of preventing older drivers from even thinking about backing up would bring about a drastic reduction in the number of accidents our generation is involved in. However, body shop owners would undoubtedly lobby against such a requirement.

The bane of all teenagers for many years was to have to parallel park while enduring the agony of testing for a license. Cars today can parallel park by themselves with absolutely no help from the driver. Now, tell the truth, how fair is this? No wonder many of today's young folks feel entitled. They have missed out on so much. How did we survive?

A common trait among most of us who belong to the human race is to engage in bizarre practices when we are faced with something that is frightening and threatens our existence. Health problems come to mind immediately. As a child, the fear of contracting something like polio or the flu was very widespread. It was particularly frightening because no one knew what caused these diseases which took millions of lives and left many who survived permanently crippled. When my father was a young man, a world-wide flu epidemic killed many millions of people. For some strange reason, in order to combat this disease, the practice of wearing something called an asphidity bag was not uncommon. This was a small cloth bag containing a mixture of vile smelling concoctions which many children were forced to wear on a string around their neck. In addition to polio and the flu, many people believed this might ward off other diseases such as asthma because the medical profession had no idea of their actual cause. Whether or not this medieval practice actually warded off any disease is left up for debate. However, it was capable of warding off friends. It was sort of a shot in the dark for desperate parents and was based on nothing but hope. As usual, most of us had no idea what was in the bag but we were painfully aware that it smelled to high heaven. In fact, anyone with a functioning olfactory system was also aware of the smell. In any group of boys, there were generally a few asphidity victims, and those not wearing a bag around their neck had already had their sense of smell seared by the fumes emitted by the bags. Either that or they were truly desperate for friends. Most adults attempted to stay upwind of any gang of boys who might be around and we were generally treated worse than lepers. How did we survive?

The only comparison I might offer to an asphidity bag is the smell of a wet billy goat. A mature billy goat for some reason finds it necessary to urinate on his scraggly beard. Over a period of time, the goat acquires a very rank smell which is difficult to describe but is never forgotten. A skunk would find the smell of a wet billy goat extremely offensive. Thank goodness, to my knowledge, this bizarre practice has not yet been adopted by male members of the human race. I am quite sure it would be frowned on in polite society and create more of a gap between men and the remainder of mankind. Instead, many of my gender have chosen to cover their bodies with strange script and drawings in the form of tattoos. As a matter of fact, discriminating billy goats would be embarrassed to be seen in the company of some of the walking billboards parading through Wal-Mart stores across this country. My question is, is it polite to attempt to read what is tattooed on the body of these people while casually gliding past pushing a shopping cart? Our parents tried to teach us that it is not polite to stare. Those of us who are naïve enough to wonder what is written on their bodies are caught between the proverbial rock and a hard place.

My mother was a firm believer in the power of another vile smelling product called Musterole. This extremely toxic agent would make today's topically applied crèmes seem as harmless as Vaseline. The environmental safety folks today would label it as toxic and require Hazmat suits for anyone in close proximity. Supposedly, the stuff was intended for those suffering from chest congestion or whooping cough and was generally applied to the chest area. The fumes wafting from the chest to the nostrils on their way to the lungs would burn away any congestion it might encounter along the way. There were occasions when my body was so slathered by this greasy mess it was difficult to keep from sliding out of my bed. The Musterole treatment by itself was painful enough, but my mother added another cruel twist. She would heat a towel in the oven almost to the point of it bursting into flames. At that point, it was slapped on top of the thick layer of Musterole already simmering and bubbling on my frail body. The heat and fumes combined to create a miniature volcanic explosion in my young nose, which frequently rendered the patient unconscious. How did we survive?

To all appearances, at least from the view point of the patient, the home remedy for virtually every sickness, disease, or accident involved as much pain as the sickness, disease, or accident which it purported to treat. There was no such thing as a curative measure which did not involve a great deal of pain. More often than not, the patient was supposed to be content with the reassuring words, "You'll feel better when it stops burning." This was frequently the case when a scrapped knee or elbow was liberally doused with alcohol, which was cheap and plentiful. If, for some reason, alcohol was deemed insufficient, the terrible tandem of Mercurochrome or Merthiolate was always somewhere in the medicine cabinet. Cremation of the skin was not the only thing they had in common. It seems that mercury was a common ingredient in both medicines, and this compound has since been shown to destroy brain cells. Unfortunately, the term "mercury poisoning" was not yet a part of our vocabulary and maybe that explains why we often broke open a thermometer and used the mercury inside to create a very shiny and slick surface on nickels, dimes and quarters. Unbeknownst to us, our brains had already been affected by the liberal application of the two twin killers and a little more mercury wouldn't hurt. Also, the rumor was that these slick, shiny coins could fool the mechanism inside a coke machine into disgorging both a coke and the coins because they were too slippery to be trapped by the coin catcher inside the machine. This tidbit of petty larceny came to me second-hand, probably from one of my older brothers or one of their friends.

Both Mercurochrome and Methiolate had the appearance of blood and the impact of a blow torch. Application was always followed by the immortal words, "Blow on it and it will stop hurting." Statements such as these caused generations of kids to lose faith in anything coming from the mouth of a parent. This loss of credibility comes back to haunt the parent later when the kid matures into a teenager and immediately categorizes all parental counseling as "pure poppycock." How did we survive?

If these practices weren't enough to send us to an early grave, the city of Florence actively engaged in a practice which added another lethal poison to the mercury already fogging our brains. In an effort to curb the mosquito population, the city regularly sent a truck around town equipped with a tank and spray which propelled clouds of dichlorodiphenyltrichloroethane into roadside ditches. This extremely long and difficult to pronounce word is just another way to say DDT. This seemed like a harmless enough practice at the time, except many of the boys my age took great delight in following the truck around the neighborhood sort of using the DDT spray to take a shower. Little did we, or anyone else at the time, know that the substance was not only lethal to mosquitos but it also caused all kinds of bad things to happen to the human body and other living organisms. It was banned for use as a spray because it was suspected of being partly responsible for the unfortunate demise of our national bird, the bald eagle. The DDT made its way into the streams and rivers and into the fish which were the main food source of the eagles. In a way, the kids of my community were probably saved from extinction because DDT made eagles unable to lay viable eggs. How did we survive?

Some of the more odious health care products of my childhood have now either been banned or are probably sold only in back alleys across the nation. One of the more popular ones was a product called Hadacol. This was a tonic which supposedly had restorative powers for a variety of ills. As I recall, it was advertised as a cure for "tired blood." It seemed to be very popular around our house as well as in many parts of the south where the public sale of liquor was banned, both morally and legally. The fact that Hadacol contained over ten percent alcohol may have contributed to its popularity.   As I recall the television commercials, the target audience seemed to be women. Very few women worked outside the home during that time, and television as we know it today was years in the future. Maintaining a household has always been a very tiring job, and no doubt all that house work could possibly cause the blood to become tired and in need of relief of some kind. If it took something like Hadacol to keep the blood pumping, so be it. It was much more acceptable in a social sense to send your kid to the East Florence Drug Store for a bottle of Hadacol than to send him to the local bootlegger for a pint of hooch. However, the two products were amazingly alike with similar results.

One final note before we move on from the topic of Hadacol. There was actually a song about the product and it was not in an advertisement. It was sung in honky-tonks around the city and people actually danced to the music. Noted author Rick Bragg writes in his book about the life of Jerry Lee Lewis that the piano player/singer once ran away from his home in Northeastern Louisiana and made his way to Bourbon Street in New Orleans. It should be mentioned Lewis was only 16 at the time. He performed an impromptu audition at a Bourbon Street honky-tonk by singing and playing the song "Hadacol Boogie." Some of the more memorable lyrics include:

> *If your radiator leaks and your motor stands still,*
>
> *Give'er Hadacol and watch her boogie up the hill,*
>
> *She'll do the Hadacol boogie.*

How did we survive?

Another product from my childhood which, surprisingly, remains on the market today is the dreaded cod-liver-oil. If anything would gag a maggot, this vile liquid certainly fit the description. It is supposedly a nutritional supplement squeezed from the liver of the poor cod fish. Initially, it was manufactured by filling large vats with the liver from freshly caught cod fish, adding some seawater and then allowing the mixture to just sit and simmer for a year before removing the oil to be bottled and sold. The manufacturing process certainly goes a long way toward explaining the taste. This method literally screamed for a better way to do things even if it involved government intervention. One would hope that the same product sold today is produced under less medieval and more modern quality control methods. Other uses for this fetid and loathsome extract from cod liver is as a base for paint and a punishment for condemned prisoners in lieu of the death penalty. Even though the fish was an unwilling participant in this whole sorry debacle, to this very day, I refuse to partake of the flesh of any fish which might have been swimming in the same ocean as a cod. How did we survive?

My mother seemed to have a feel for medicine which was not only toxic but later found totally unacceptable to federal agencies which oversee such products. Paregoric was another one of her favorite medicinal products which later fell on bad times. I can remember that she always kept a bottle handy and force fed it to us when we had an upset stomach or some other ailment which had an unknown origin. It seemed to have a calming effect and the reason was that later research showed it contained a considerable amount of opium. Under today's laws, thousands of innocent mothers across this country could have been prosecuted as drug users and for child abuse. How did we survive?

It has not escaped my attention that there seems to be an ongoing dispute between adults and the condition of the hair on the head of their teenage sons. This dispute can range from not being enough hair to the extreme opposite of being too much hair. Any kid growing up in the fifties and sixties with what passes for hair today would have had to fight their way to and from school every day. In addition, a head showing only scraps of multi-colored hair here and there would have immediately been diagnosed as a bad case of mange and treated accordingly. It was not uncommon to see dogs with mange skulking around the community, and most parents had a horror of their children contracting the dreaded condition.

Most general stores carried a product specifically for mange which was, for the sake of clarity, called "mange dip." The chemical was mixed with water and dogs were frequently subjected to an unwelcome dousing in a large foot tub or barrel. Kids and dogs with a confirmed case of mange were generally not welcome in finer homes around the community.

A friend of mine once accidentally drank a large gulp from a jar of mange dip and swallowed it before he could stop himself. He was doing some odd jobs for a lady and sent his helper to get his water jar from another room before they took a break. His water jar was actually nothing more than a quart Mason jar, but it served the purpose very well. Unbeknownst to his helper, he went to the wrong room where the house owner kept an identical Mason jar with leftover mange dip sitting on the counter. My friend, being hot and thirsty, took what he called, a "big swig" before realizing the liquid rushing toward his stomach was definitely not one hundred percent water. A quick call to the doctor brought forth some sterling advice. He was wisely informed not to drink anymore of the mange dip but instead follow up with large volumes of water. He did so and lived to tell about it. Apparently, the product was far more lethal to the tiny skin mites which cause mange than to the digestive tract of humans.

The other side of the hair controversy involves too much hair and a fierce determination not to part with one single milli-meter of its length. I know this to be true because our two teen-age grandsons have a head of hair which would make Bigfoot proud. Any suggestion by their parents to have it trimmed makes the NRA's on-going defense of the Second Amendment seem like playing patty-cake at a little girl's tea party. There was no such controversy or discussion about hair length while growing up in my daddy's house. The simple statement, "You boys go down to Nick's today and get a haircut," cut straight to the core of the matter, and we knew the debate was over before it actually began. For the most part, our daddy tolerated very little debate on any subject. Nick was the barber located in the heart of East Florence and probably removed more hair from heads than Geronimo and his entire wild bunch of Apaches combined. Apparently, we were not trusted to pay for the transaction because Daddy never gave us the money to do so. All his sons had somehow picked up the odious habit of purchasing cigarettes with any loose change which happened to wind up in their pockets. Therefore, it was always necessary for him to handle all financial transactions in person. He always stopped by on his way home from work, and woe be to any of us if Nick told him that he had not laid eyes on us for a while.

In addition to being the village barber, so to speak, the bench on the sidewalk outside of Nick's was the gathering place for the old men of the community who had nothing else to do. Many of them paid Nick twenty five cents for the use of his shower in the back room. Included with this price was the use of a bar of soap and a semi-clean towel. My own grandfather often took advantage of this deal and was one of Nick's frequent customers.

There is another side to this coin which has gradually occurred to me over the last few years. It was during this time I discovered it is much more pleasant to have my hair cut by a pretty woman than a smelly man who generally reeks of tobacco, liquor, or Old Spice. Also, women barbers never want to argue about politics. This newly acquired practice places me in a quandary because I never know whether to say I am going to the barber shop or the beauty shop. While sitting in the beauty shop waiting my turn in the chair, I have discovered that the conversation between the men customers during my vulnerable teenage years was nothing compared to the tidbits I pick up around a bunch of females. Sometimes I become annoyed because all the hair dryers tend to drown out the really good parts of the conversation, and I am left with only fragments and have to imagine the rest. Also, women apparently put a lot more emphasis on getting a haircut than men normally do. This is not universally true, because I know a lot of men who are quite vain about their hair. But, for the most part, men and boys are generally forced by their mother or their wife to have this chore taken care of. For example, recently I walked in and was able to go directly to the empty chair. While sitting there I overheard the barbers, or whatever, talking about the lady who was driving out of the parking lot just as I came into the building. From what I could gather, the lady told them she had passed out three times already and was rather woozy when she got up out of the chair to leave and had to sit down for a few minutes. During the conversation they happened to mention the lady's name, so I checked the obituaries the next few days to determine if she was still alive. There are very few men in this world who are that determined to get a haircut.

Less than a half block from Nick's barber shop was a den of iniquity Daddy sternly lectured each of his son's never to be seen inside of or even in close proximity: the infamous poolroom. It was Daddy's opinion that only lowlifes and other degenerates would hang out in such a place. Later, as a teenager and allowed to drive, my warped sense of reasoning interpreted Daddy's warning in a very strict sense and, instead, hung out in a pool room uptown. In addition to the atmosphere, they served the best burgers in town. This bit of subterfuge allowed me to honestly answer in the negative anytime he questioned me about hanging out in the poolroom in East Florence. This is irrefutable evidence that the brain and resulting thought patterns of a teenager will never be fully understood and parents can only hope their kids survive those fateful years.

My hair care experience became much less structured when we moved from East Florence to our home in the Central community of rural Lauderdale County. My maturity level was sufficient enough to decide for myself my hair style and who would cut it. The closest barber shop to my house was in a small building only a couple of miles from our house. Unlike my former barber where three chairs were frequently in operation at the same time, this was strictly a one chair operation. The time period was during the early sixties when hair styles in some parts of the country became so outlandish they defied description. This counter culture craze never touched the doorstep at my new barber's establishment. The long-haired, make love not war, zealot would not have received a friendly reception from the barber or the clientele. In the parking lot outside, there was a hunting rifle in the back window of every pick-up and probably a .38 Special under the front seat.

The fellow in charge specialized in the traditional style of the day, which was the comb-over favored by so many of the older generation of the community. For some reason, older guys with only a few strands of hair believed they could ward off total baldness by combing the few remaining strands across the top of their head to the other side. This deception is impossible to cover up but continues to this very day. Apparently, this partially bald condition is also accompanied by two other dreaded afflictions. One is obviously total deafness, which mercifully shields the man in question from the snickers and snide remarks made by those in close proximity. The other has to be none other than, at best, partial blindness. No one in their right mind with eyes to see would wear their hair like that. The only explanation is that they are not able to see how ridiculous they look.

The style of the day for teenage boys became the flat top which did present some problems for the barber. My knowledge of the barbering business is very limited to this day and consists entirely of the accumulation of assorted bits of knowledge gained from about twenty minutes in the chair about once per month. However, in my humble opinion, the essence of the successful flat top was concentrated on the top of the head. The sides of the head were simply buzzed cut and required no particular skill. However, for a flat top to comply with its name, the top must, of necessity, be flat, or at least reasonably so. Also, the hair should stand perfectly upright in order to maintain that look so desired by its adherents. This was the only problem the fellow had in perfecting the flat top: he had considerable trouble maintaining the preferred level of flatness. In order to do so, he would get right in the face of the customer in the chair and use his eyes sort of like a carpenter's level and eye-ball his handiwork. The problems generally began at this point, because he would begin to trim the high side which soon resulted in it becoming the low side. The inevitable result of his constant tweaking from side to side soon caused the flat top to become a burr head. It should go without saying that the burr head look was not cool for teenage boys during the 1960s.

There was a very simple solution to the problem generated by hair which refused to stand upright. Fortunately for teenage boys, there was a product on the market called Butch Wax. This very popular staple was packaged in small, round jars and had the consistency of molasses in February. Applying ample amounts of this material forced even the laziest strand into a vertical position until the next washing. Too much Butch Wax often created a wall of hair which required a pre-wash with a liberal amount of mineral spirits before water could have any effect. Another down-side to using Butch Wax was that one's head became sort of like the sticky paper hung up in barns and houses to attract and kill flies. Flying insects frequently became stuck in the hair and the teenage boy with the cool flattop became a laughingstock among his dopey friends.

Many teenage boys converted to the flat top after years of the little boy comb-overs which seemed to be mandated by mothers nationwide. A sure sign of independence among boys is when the mother loses control over her son's hair. As long as she can comb his hair over to one side while cooing about his good looks, the boy is still under her control. Like puppies and baby goats, cute little boys soon grow into something ugly and unrecognizable.

Many boys had a cowlick which refused to be trained to go along with the rest of the hair and was a constant irritant to the women in our lives, mainly our mothers. The remedy for this problem was another hair care product called Brylcreem. Brylcreem was basically composed of oil pumped directly from the ground, which was heavy enough to whip the nastiest cowlick into submission. Continued application caused the hair to have a tendency to just sort of lay over on its side from nothing but sheer exhaustion. Brylcreem had one of the catchiest jingles of all time. It went something like this:

Brylcreem, a little dab'll do ya,

Use more, only if you dare.

But, watch out, The gal's will all pursue ya,

They love to run their fingers through your hair.

Not only was this pure rubbish as far as attracting members of the opposite sex, but, once locked into your brain, it was impossible to dislodge this ridiculous tune without consulting a medium. Nevertheless, a liberal application of Butch Wax would immediately negate the effects of years of weighting the hair down with Brylcreem. It would cause even the laziest strand of hair to stand at attention like a U. S. Marine on a recruiting poster.

So, for the princely sum of fifty-cents, one could obtain a haircut as well as pick up a great deal of knowledge listening to the constant conversation between the barber and whoever was in the chair at the time. There is no doubt that heads were cut that even a rusty curry comb would find distasteful. It wasn't a big deal at the time, but it was not uncommon to hear him point out the presence of lice on a customer's head. This was a service not many of today's cosmetologists would be willing to perform for their customers, but at this place the service was provided at no charge. Not only was a flat top the essence of style, it required virtually no maintenance and deprived the little gray back critters of a place to hide.

One day while awaiting my turn in the chair, the relatively quiet atmosphere in the little building was interrupted by the agonizing scream of a rather large man in the chair. He ripped the protective sheet from around his neck, jumped from the chair and used some rather colorful language to describe the fellow's clumsy use of his giant Oster clippers. It seems the customer was a pulp wood cutter by profession and had acquired a rather large wad of pine tree resin which had become entangled in his long and unkempt hair. At the time the barber was either conveying or mining for information and failed to notice the obstruction as he chatted amicably with others waiting their turn in his chair. Everything came to a screeching halt when his clippers plowed headlong into the unyielding mass of resin which ripped hair follicles out by the dozens from the man's scalp. The indignant customer not only questioned his hair cutting ability as well as his parentage, but stomped out the door without paying. This was good stuff for a rather naïve teenage boy.

My new barber was possessed with a quick wit, and snappy comebacks were not uncommon. On one occasion, a fellow from outside the community had somehow managed to locate the shop in order to take advantage of a fifty-cent haircut. He was undoubtedly fleeing the high-priced barbers in town which was not uncommon. During the usual back-and-forth banter between barber and customer, the new customer casually asked if he had "lived in this area his entire life?" Without missing a snip, he responded, "not yet." You can't make this stuff up. In today's world of non-stop reality television shows, this one-man hair cutting operation would have been a slam-dunk star.

It is not difficult for me to send young people into a zombie-like state today. All it takes is to launch into a spiel of how different things were when I was growing up. They really have no interest in what it was like to have a dial telephone on a party line with four other families. Even more confusing would be the ring pattern which differentiated one household from another. For example, if four families shared the same line, there had to be some method of informing one family the phone call was for them and not any of the others on the same line. People picking up the phone when others were already talking could lead to serious disputes and that was often the case. It is quite possible that disputes over telephone priorities caused more hard feelings than property lines and the relative worth of a hunting dog. Therefore, each household had a distinct ring pattern. It might be two long rings and one short. Or, two short rings and one long or any other combination. Thus, the phrase, "that's our ring, answer the phone," was often heard and understood by everyone in the house.

For young folks today, the concept of having to wait to use their own telephone is as foreign as standing in line at a telephone booth. They can take their smart phone and call downtown London in a few seconds and have no idea or appreciation that my bag phone upstairs in the attic was the grandfather of that miracle of communication. The cell phone they grew up with is capable of taking photographs and transmitting them around the world in a matter of seconds. One of the miracles of my childhood was to see and hold in my hand a paper photograph that was developed inside of a Polaroid Land camera in just a matter of minutes. The fact that this wonderful device was capable of such a miracle without first taking the undeveloped film to the drug store and then waiting days for the actual picture has no place in their world. The only drawback to the modern system is that families will no longer have a cigar box or a shoe box full of cherished photographs to pass on to their children. Some of my most revered possessions are the old faded photographs of loved ones packed away in an upstairs closet. Memories stored only on a gadget the size of a baby's thumbnail lose a lot of meaning.

Hopefully, all those smart people have already solved this problem and the solution, like many other things, has been lost somewhere in my brain. Maybe, when all these brilliant young folks are older, technology will have advanced to the point their smart phone will draw laughs and blank stares from their grandchildren.

All of us have experienced the annoying call during supper trying to sell us something or solicit donations for a worthy cause. Growing up, there was no such thing as a recorded voice on the telephone instructing the listener to stay on the line for a very important message. Such an occurrence would have frightened the daylights out of us. Instead, actual people came to our home and attempted to sell us something in person. They were called traveling salesmen. As far as I can remember, these folks were always men and therefore there is no need for me to use the preferred unisex term of sales person. The robo-calls we get today are far less annoying than the knock at the door during the middle of the day. Invariably, standing at the door was a total stranger intent on selling us insurance, a set of Fuller brushes, a Bible, a Hoover vacuum cleaner, or a set of encyclopedias: World Book, Britannica or Compton's, which was simply Britannica with pictures, to be more specific. Untold numbers of parents spent money they did not yet have in order to buy a set of these encyclopedias with the high hope their child would be spared the drudgery of a low-paying job with no future.

Surely, the advent of on-line purchasing and next day delivery by Amazon has rendered these professions obsolete. Generations of college students have missed out on a wonderful opportunity to not only travel but to earn a few dollars in the process. How did we survive?

During my childhood there were many services provided for folks that were just a part of doing business at the time. There was no extra charge. One of these was the full service attendant at most gas stations. Generations have matured without the luxury of stopping to buy gas and have an attendant come to your car and pump the gas for you. In addition, the attendant washed your windshield and checked under the hood for adequate oil and other fluid levels. He also checked the tires and provided air if necessary. While I was in college, my daddy ran a little country store after he retired from TVA. He sold mostly gas and groceries. Running a country store by itself is not a problem, nor is running a gas station a problem. The problems arise when your business enterprise is both a country store and a gas station. One person cannot reasonably provide service inside the store and outside at the pumps at the same time. Therefore, help is necessary and that is where I came on the scene. I was his full service attendant. All the above were part of my duties in addition to carrying bags of groceries to the car for women. Rain or shine, I was always on the alert for customers pulling up to the two pumps in front of his store building. This job taught me humility which I sorely needed at the time. Many folks can be mighty picky at times, even when they are the recipient of a free service. Missing a spot on the windshield, sloshing a little gas on the fender or causing a customer to have to wait was often sufficient cause enough for a good reprimand. The fact that my daddy ran a gas station came in handy during the gas shortage of the 1970s. I traveled from home to Tuscaloosa with enough gas in five gallon cans in my trunk to be considered a hazard.

Inside the store, many of the customers did not pay but told Daddy just to "put that down." This meant to add whatever they had purchased to their ticket, and they would pay at the end of the month. Most actually paid but when Daddy sold the store he was owed hundreds of dollars by folks who never paid. The concept of skipping out on a legitimate debt is apparently one which will never disappear from the scene no matter how many generations have come and gone.

My daddy did something most small country stores did not do and that was to provide S & H Green Stamps with every purchase. These little stamps, which resembled a postage stamp, could be redeemed for such things as toasters, lamps, blenders, radios, and literally thousands of other products. The customer moistened the back and attached the stamps to pages in the little collection book also provided by the retailer. Obviously, the higher the price tag for the item the more books required for redemption. The end purpose was to try to ensure customer loyalty and get the folks addicted to get what they considered to be "free stuff" from the very colorful and attractive catalog. Plaid Stamps and Top Value Stamps were also in the market and competed for business with Green Stamps. Collecting and redeeming stamps was very popular by many retailers for a good while, but most of the stamp companies went out of business in the 1970s. No doubt, there are still countless books of unredeemed stamps tucked away in the sock drawer of many of our senior citizens just waiting for a comeback.

The rapid rise of machinery to do the work formerly accomplished by sheer brawn has taken away golden opportunities for adults to impress upon the younger generation the importance of toeing the line. As a boy, it was a common sight to see gangs of men digging ditches with picks and shovels along roads and construction sites. Parents and teachers used visual aids such as these to try and stress the importance of getting what they called, "a good education." A poor report card was always reason to bring out the, "you'll wind up digging ditches" refrain in an attempt to scare youngsters into hitting the books. In addition, occasionally a gang of men seen working would be chained together. They were prisoners and this form of hard labor was part of the punishment for their crime. The notorious "chain gangs" of my childhood have long since been banned as cruel and unusual punishment, but they provided parents a good teaching tool for their wide-eyed children with their nose pressed to the backseat window as the car slowly moved past the sad looking group swinging picks and shovels.

Of course, modern earth moving equipment can move more dirt in an hour than a gang of men could accomplish in days. This needed improvement has given adults less ammunition on the subject. The fact is that operators of these machines earn more per hour than the Classical Greek Poetry, Art History, and Physical Education majors working in the check-out line at Wal-Mart can only visualize in their dreams. Maybe some of the Harvard graduates playing the piccolo in New York subways should have taken a couple of vocational courses in high school. Actually, my childhood dream occupation, outside of garbage collector, was to be an elevator operator. The thought of wearing that snazzy outfit while sitting in the corner and ordering people around inside an elevator was somehow attractive to me. Unfortunately, that particular employment opportunity went the way of the juke box and mimeograph repairman. Who would have thought?

The truth is that every generation thinks their time spent growing up was so much better than that of other generations. This was true when I was a boy, and it will be true until "the cows come home" as my daddy was fond of saying. It is my fervent hope and prayer that my grandchildren and their grandchildren have growing up experiences they consider far better than mine. It would truly be a shame if all the good times were already used up.

*****

Jackie Hastings

Hummers

The early morning and late afternoon hours between early April and early October are always among my favorite times around home. This is when the hummingbirds return from their long winter visit to warmer southern climates and come back to our house to spend the summer. We eagerly anticipate their return, because the arrival of the hummingbirds heralds the coming of spring just as much as the red buds, dogwoods, and buttercups. It is certainly a blessing to share a wonderful time of the year with such a beautiful little bird. I have been told they return to the area of their birthplace, but I have no way of knowing if that is true. If it is true then hummingbirds, like so many of God's creatures, consider home to be a very special place. We hope they are as happy to be at our house as we are to have them.

The soft humming noise of their tiny wings is calming to my soul at the beginning or end of a busy day. While we are sitting on our deck or back porch, they are very close at hand and easily observed while they feed. We have kept a record of their arrival and departure times for a good while now and they are very consistent year after year. The first one always arrives about the first week of April. Two or three others will soon join the first arrival, and they will spend a few days feeding together.

Soon they all seem to disappear and there will be very little sign whatsoever of any of them for a week or so. It is my guess they are building a nest, but I am not sure. Sometimes, during the winter after all the leaves have fallen, I run across one of the tiny nests and it is a work of art. To fly so far just to build something so small is a miracle in itself.

Shortly, there will be hummers aplenty and their numbers will continue to increase as the summer passes. They soon become so numerous they are impossible for our eyes to count. The little critters zip and zoom all around us, and near misses are not uncommon. Low level, supersonic flights across our deck make us want to duck, but they are gone before we can react. Believe it or not, many people have something akin to a morbid fear of these tiny bullets with feathers. A fellow at church absolutely refuses to go anywhere around a humming-bird because he is afraid of being speared by their beak. The odds of this happening are impossible for me to calculate, but they must be about the same as being devoured by a killer whale while standing on the bank alongside Cypress Creek. This guy is missing a real treat!

Early morning and late afternoon are their favorite feeding times. I have read that they normally feed every ten minutes or so because of an extremely high metabolic rate. They certainly seem to use up a lot of energy as they fly lickety-split around us and disappear in a blink over the trees in our yard. Toward the end of September, we have estimated a hundred or more are jockeying for their turn to sip the sweet nectar from the feeders, apparently fueling up for what lies ahead. My wife prepares this mixture constantly and buys so much sugar that she could be easily mistaken for a moonshiner. Law enforcement people frequently get a lead on moonshiners because they buy a lot of sugar, which is essential to brew their own brand of nectar. Margo often has to refill the six to eight feeders every day. The recipe she has always used consists of one part sugar to three parts water without any heating. She adds no coloring to the mixture and the birds seem to relish it. Some claim the mixture must be tinted red to attract the birds, but that is not the case at our house. However, I do frequently see an obviously confused bird buzzing around some kind of red object we might have hanging on the back porch.

Around the first of October their numbers begin to dwindle rapidly, and the last ones generally will leave by the middle of the month. There is a place a few miles south of our house on the Natchez Trace where the birds supposedly gather by the thousands before they leave for warmer temperatures. It is a beaver pond surrounded by jewel weed, which is supposedly a favorite for hummers. My wife and I have visited there several times in the fall, but on the days we were there, we actually observed fewer birds than at our house. As with a lot of other things in life, timing is everything.

We often find ourselves between the proverbial rock and a hard place when they begin their fall exodus. Some so-called experts say to leave a feeder out as long as even one bird continues to feed. We have chosen the other path. There have been times when we have had to bring in the last feeder to encourage the stragglers to leave and get on the road before really cold weather arrives. The few slackers that hang around too long remind me of some people I have known who insisted on putting things off until the last minute. There are times in the life of a hummingbird and in the life of people when waiting too long to act can have very serious consequences.

Just as their arrival in the spring signals the beginning of warm weather, their departure in late fall is a harbinger of the winter that is well on the way. It is always a sad time to see them leave, but they have places to go and things to do and we are only spectators enjoying the show. I have read they journey to Mexico and South America to winter, flying across the Gulf of Mexico in flocks too large to count. That seems like a mighty long and treacherous journey for such a tiny creature. The Bible tells us that God will not put a task before us without also providing the strength to achieve it. He obviously does the same for hummingbirds.

During the first few weeks they are in residence, the birds are extremely cantankerous. They fight constantly and try to bully other birds away from the feeders. Sometimes one bird will stay close to the feeders just for the sole purpose of driving the others away. Even when there are only five or six birds and dozens of feeding holes available, their greed seems to know no end. However, toward the end of their stay, they calm down and become less hostile to each other. Occasionally, many birds can be seen feeding together at the same feeder with no bickering or bullying.

Their behavior reminds me a lot of people and the way we behave toward each other. During my professional career as a school counselor, I worked with young people from kindergarten through high school, and it seemed that far too much of my time was spent attempting to settle squabbles between folks. The consequences of the same type behavior by adults can be viewed every day on the evening news. People and hummingbirds seem to have a problem sharing things with others. Whether it is food, space, land, or friends, there never seems to be enough to go around. The fact of the matter is that there is always plenty, we just tend to want more than our fair share. I have known people who did not want to own all the land, just everything that touches what they already possessed. When a hummingbird leaves our home they travel light because it is obvious they can take nothing with them on the long journey ahead. Wouldn't it be great if people could learn the same lesson?

There are many wonderful truths taught in the Bible and one of the simplest is what we have come to call the Golden Rule: that is to treat others like we would have them treat us.

Most of us have been taught that rule from early childhood and most of us continue to ignore it until the day we die. It has always amazed me how some folks treat others, but at least the lawyers are able to make a good living and profit from man's inhumanity to his fellow man. Early in life, we are frequently competitive and egotistical to a fault. We thrive on multi-tasking, clattering cell phones, driving fast, and keeping others away from what we have accumulated solely for ourselves. The way many of us lead our lives is a perfect prescription for hypertension and a life cut short by a stroke or heart attack.

As I have grown older, I find myself less annoyed by what I consider to be the failings of others and have actually concluded that many of my problems have been the result of my own shortcomings and not the fault of others. It seems to be much easier at this stage of my life to ignore things which were once of great importance in my life. Maybe I have finally seen that the log in my own eye prevents me from seeing the splinter in the eye of my neighbor as it teaches in the Bible. Things that were once the centerpiece of my life have slipped so far down my list they have no priority whatsoever. I often wonder why they were so important to me at one time. Constantly bickering with those around us will not come close to solving the problems we will face on this earth. Surely, life has more in store for us than never-ending conflict. It saddens me to see families and relationships consumed by this type behavior. The Bible tells us that in the grand scheme of things, our lives are like a puff of smoke that appears and quickly dissolves. Like the hummingbirds at our house they are there only for a quick visit and then go away to another place. It has been said many times that life is too short and it slips away fast enough as it is. There is enough misery in this world to go around without folks spending precious time trying to create more. Unfortunately, it has taken me far too long to realize this is true and live my own life accordingly. Enjoying what the Lord has given me, even though

I deserve none of it, is more important than ever before. Surely, God doesn't bless us just so we can grow fat and lazy and fight over table scraps. We have an obligation to use His blessings for purposes other than our own. Could it really be true that God places us on this earth for a deeper reason than to blithely spend what little time we have being selfish?

Maybe people and hummingbirds realize late in the game there is a long hard journey ahead, and we must prepare ourselves for it. It is easy to see evidence that the hummingbirds are preparing for their long journey and, unfortunately, not so easy to see similarly intense preparation in people. The hummingbirds have figured out the good life does not last forever. There will not always be someone around willing to mix up unlimited amounts of sweet nectar to get us through the day. We have a responsibility not only to ourselves but to others around us. We must be helpers and not just takers. Just think of the wonderful difference it would make in this world if we lived our lives with that thought in mind.

God certainly created a wide variety of critters to live together on this earth. There is no doubt that each has a purpose and a reason for being here. Sometimes, in my ignorance, this purpose and reason is difficult for me to grasp, particularly if it tends to run counter to my own convenience and comfort. Why an all-knowing God decided to create ticks, copperheads, and moles is far beyond my feeble ability to understand. On the other hand, the Bible tells us that His ways are not our ways and His thoughts are higher than our own. But, when I listen to a mockingbird sing or watch the flight of a hummingbird, I know instantly they are here to enhance our lives, even if it is only for a short time.

Preparation for what is to come might be one thing we could learn from one of God's smallest creatures. The hummingbirds know our house is not their final home. They are only visiting for a short time and then they are gone. The same is true of all the inhabitants of this earth, even humans. Our lives will be much richer if we learned this lesson sooner rather than later.

******

Hunting Tales

There are many pursuits in life which require a great deal of skill in order to be successful. Activities such as brain surgery, cooking something "fit to eat" as folks say around here, higher mathematics, bridge-building, quilting, and piloting an airliner all come to mind as areas where a great deal of ability is necessary. Disaster is just around the corner if those engaging in these activities have not trained properly and achieved a certain level of expertise. A friend of mine says that some activities require proficiency from the "neck up" while others are from the "neck down." Those listed above can definitely be categorized as "neck up" type skills because each involves the use of a great deal of gray matter.

On the other hand, there are activities of a different nature which require little or no skill, but success is achieved strictly by chance, or luck, as some might say. Some examples might be playing the slots, picking a spouse, surviving on an interstate highway, being customer number one million to visit a store, and being elected to public office. When luck makes one successful, it is often called "defying the odds." It has been my experience that a small number of folks seem to be born with some sort of intangibility which allows them to defy the odds on a regular basis. They have the luck of the mythical character

King Midas where everything they touch turns to gold. Others spend their entire life looking for that one lucky break which never comes. The never-ending search for that lucky break has made casino owners incredibly wealthy. A friend claims to have made a small fortune at a casino but the problem with that was he left home with a large fortune. But, on rare occasions, the table is turned and luck trumps skill, but not very often.

Take hunting for example. There is absolutely no doubt that for a hunter to be successful on a regular basis, a great deal of skill is necessary. I have friends who are ardent deer and turkey hunters. The calendar year for them is divided into two parts: hunting season and the rest of the year. Only events of enormous magnitude can deflect some of these guys from squeezing every possible second out of a hunting season. Virtually nothing is allowed to stand in their way. The anticipation of Christmas as a child is nothing compared to the sheer joy a dedicated hunter feels as the season slowly approaches. Molasses on a cold February morning moves at the speed of quicksilver compared to the tortoise-like approach of opening day as the days on the calendar are slowly counted down.

During hunting season the poor wives of these zealots are forced to take up knitting, sign up for Polka lessons, and actually read cook books to fill in the long hours they spend alone at home. Prisoners who are kept in solitary confinement have more companionship than these neglected women when hunting season is in full blast. Pity the poor hunter, or fisherman for that matter, whose spouse requires their presence around the house on a predictable and regular basis. One or the other is up the proverbial creek without a paddle. The choice they frequently make does not necessarily lead to marital bliss. In a lot of cases, their hunting license takes precedence over their marriage license.

Someone once said that if you give a man a fish you will feed him for a day. However, if you teach that man to fish, you feed him for a lifetime. The same type logic could be applied to hunting but with a slightly different twist. If you give a man a piece of tenderloin from a nice deer, that will feed him for a day. On the other hand, if you teach that same man to hunt he will immediately feel the need to purchase a high-powered rifle, a tree stand, a deluxe deer cart, a four-wheel drive ATV, a rear basket for his new four-wheel drive ATV, a trailer to transport his new four-wheel drive ATV, trail cameras, a hunting blind, a scope for his new high-powered rifle which would put the Hubble telescope to shame, a muzzle-loader and high-powered bow with enough arrows to shame an Apache raiding party, huge amounts of black gun powder, night vision goggles, an automatic feeder, binoculars, deer decoys, a GPS system, hand and foot warmers, a backpack, scent-free clothing, heated socks, heated underwear, ultra-ear hearing enhancer, a telescoping saw and tree pruner, bear defense spray, game cleaning gloves, tick spray, camo leisure suit, trail marking ribbon, camo seat covers for his truck, camo underwear, ATV harrow drag, plow, planter and disc, a meat grinder, scent killer, a taxidermy for dummies CD, several knives, boots, rangefinder, and a deer bleat and bawl call. This is only a partial list and other items must, of necessity, be purchased at a later date. This means that as soon as one of his hunting buddies gets something new he must immediately buy the same item of equal or greater value.

After a few local hunting trips, it becomes immediately apparent that the deer around home are skinny runts compared to the deer in south Alabama or the deer in Illinois. This observation could result in the purchase of a camper and a towing vehicle. Soon, his vacation days are spent hunkered down in a snow storm somewhere up north while the poor spouse is learning to play Solitaire.

It is not unusual for hunters to drive hundreds of miles simply to watch someone demonstrate a new turkey or duck call. The search for a better duck call is somewhat akin to the search for a better mouse trap; it has no end. It has been recently brought to my attention that a family in the state of Louisiana, through much diligence and hard work, has actually made a fortune with this small, simple instrument. They cost only a few cents each to make but the fellow who came up with the idea is smiling all the way to the bank while the customer is sitting in a duck blind with his feet in freezing water having the time of his life.

Some of the guys I have actually gone into the woods with carried firearms fully capable of dropping a bull elephant at a mile's distance. They wear camouflage clothing which can't be seen, heard, or smelled. Their four wheel drive vehicles will take them up the face of a cliff at interstate speed and they use scent killer that will singe the hair inside your nose and destroy olfactory glands. It could be said they are engaging in chemical warfare against the poor woodland creatures. It is nothing to them to sprinkle fox urine or skunk scent all around while sitting in a tree for hours at a time and firmly believe this is normal behavior. When they actually kill a deer they are elbow deep in guts and deer organs. Deer hunting has made outside showers popular in the homes of many hunters. Ironically, these same guys cannot change the foul-smelling diapers of their infant children without gagging or throwing up.

Prior to opening day, hours are spent in exhausting physical labor hacking away undergrowth and tree limbs to clear a firing lane from their tree stand. Meanwhile, back at home, their long abandoned wives cannot get them to even mow the grass. This tree stand then becomes their home away from home where they sit for hours in freezing weather until they are so cold, it is dangerous to attempt the climb back down. For safety purposes, it is necessary to even harness their rigid bodies to the tree so they won't topple to the ground, a practice picked up from Japanese snipers during World War II. Many more hours are spent before the season opens honing their shooting skills and prowling the woods scouting for signs of the game they are hunting. Most have erected tree stands in their yard so they can practice their bow hunting skills. The neighbors are afraid to let their children or pets venture outside. They even place cameras in the woods in order to photograph the unsuspecting critters as they travel to feed and bed down during the day. They soon become the paparazzi of the forest. These photos are then used to plot their daily movement so they can be in the right position the second the season opens. A recent advertisement in a hunting magazine offered a trail camera which would thoughtfully send to the hunter's iPhone text messages any time an unsuspecting deer passed within range of the camera lens. Technology allows the hunter to predict movement of game much like a general predicts troop movement on the battle field. During the time leading up to opening day, it is a good idea for normal people to refrain from entering the woods to answer the call of nature or engage in any other behavior you wouldn't want displayed on a hunter's trail camera.

My wife and I never wonder when hunting season begins because it sounds like a young war is breaking out all around our house when that day finally arrives. We are often forced to belly crawl to our car when we attempt to leave the house. We pondered using a white flag when we venture outside but then realized some frazzled hunter might mistake it for the tail of their favorite game, the wily white-tail deer. For this very reason, women who live in rural areas refuse to hang out their laundry during hunting season. A pair of tighty-whities could easily become a huge buck in the eyes of a desperate hunter. When all these factors come together and game is finally slung over the shoulder or lashed down to the back of a four wheel drive ATV, for the triumphant march out of the woods, it is all worthwhile.

On the other hand, pure luck sometimes trumps skill, although this is probably a very rare occurrence. When this does happen, it is as if the game seems to pursue the hunter and, after suffering a lucky shot, runs away and falls dead at the back door of the hunting lodge, so to speak.

Several instances in particular come to mind when this was almost the case: one involving me and one involving another hunter.

The latter occurred early, like about four o'clock one morning, when I was headed out to deer hunt not far from my home. I was in my truck on a very narrow, dirt road bordered on one side by a cornfield and the other side by a steep hill covered with trees. A short distance in front of me was a man in a pickup who was either on his way to deer hunt, or very lost. Other than the criminal element, who else would be out at that time of the morning?

Sometimes things happen so quickly it is difficult to comprehend what you think you are seeing with your own eyes. This was the case on this dark, cold morning in Southern Tennessee. All of a sudden a deer burst forth from the cornfield to our right and crashed head first into the side of his rear bumper. It all happened so fast it was impossible to tell if it was a buck or doe. From my perspective the deer appeared to be attacking the truck. I am sure the driver was startled and wondered what could possibly have hit his truck from the rear. By the time he had emerged from the cab, I had pulled in behind him. We met at the rear of his truck and gazed down at a very dead, hopefully, eight-point buck. I told him what I saw from my vantage point while driving behind him, and both of us just stood and sort of scratched our head. Then, inexplicably, he returned to the cab of his truck and came back with a very old military style rifle complete with bayonet. It may have been left over from the Spanish-American War or possibly World War I. He administered the coup de grace by plunging the bayonet into the buck and then turned to me and said, "I just wanted to make sure he was dead."

This was probably a good idea because very few of us want a live eight-point buck thrashing around in the bed of a truck. It could prove to be quite dangerous. Actually, my experience has been that any sort of wildlife in the open bed of a truck is dangerous. A few years back, I ran over a large rattlesnake and, thinking it was dead, tossed it into the bed of my truck to take home to remove the skin and rattles. I must admit, I also relished the thought of my wife's reaction when she discovered her idiot husband had a rattlesnake in his truck. Much to my surprise, when I arrived back at the house the reptile was not dead but very much alive and very angry. Apparently, rattlesnakes do not enjoy a leisurely ride in the bed of a truck. Thank goodness I had the foresight to toss it into the bed of the truck and not the cab. Facing a rattlesnake in the woods might be a normal situation, but dispatching one in the bed of a pickup was a new experience. Suffice it to say, an irate rattlesnake coiled up in the corner of a pickup bed is a worthy opponent. I have always heard it is not a good idea to shoot a snake which happens to drop from a limb into your boat while fishing, and it is an equally bad idea to shoot a formerly dead snake which you foolishly tossed into the bed of your nice pickup truck. Insurance will not cover the resulting damage to the sheet metal, and the agent might somehow get it into his head that you are a poor risk and possibly not insurable.

So, while the hunter's action with the bayonet seemed cold and heartless, it did make a lot of sense to me. After helping him load the deer into his truck, each of us headed our separate way. He turned around and headed back home because his hunt for the day was over before mine had even begun. I spent most of the rest of the morning thinking how wonderful it would have been if I had been able to astonish my hunting companions with my tale of bringing down an eight point buck with a bayonet before the hunt actually began. A few seconds can make all the difference in the world when it comes to being in the right place at the right time or the wrong place at the wrong time for that matter. Lives and reputations have been irrevocably changed by both.

During a conversation with an older friend many years ago, he happened to mention he had eaten quite a few ground-hogs back in the day and found them mighty tasty. My experience has been that the phrase "back in the day" is over-used and is hard to pin down the exact day something took place. The mere fact our conversation had drifted to such an obscure topic is all the evidence needed to understand why I am never invited to parties where the invitees stand around and make small talk. It is quite possible many in polite society would be offended by subject matter I consider to be quite interesting. Be that as it may, these large, furry critters have several aliases. They are often referred to as ground squirrels or woodchucks. In fact, it is the very same varmint from my childhood which has inspired one of the most perplexing questions of all time and would continue to confound kids today if they would only turn their smartphones off:

How much wood would a woodchuck chuck if a woodchuck could chuck wood? As much wood as a woodchuck would if a wood-chuck could chuck wood.

Believe it or not, kids my age frequently entertained our-selves by reciting these silly tongue twisters and were somehow under the illusion we were actually having fun.

In our part of the world these members of the marmot family have been known to destroy well-kept lawns and play havoc with soybean and corn crops, not to mention their annoy-ing habit of finding wood trim on houses and barns quite tasty. Their burrows are large and have several escape tunnels which only compound the damage. Over the years, several of my not-too-smart friends have shown up with their eyebrows burned off and a red, peeling face showing the results of their failed attempt to destroy a groundhog burrow and, obviously, the critter residing in such a burrow. Their anger and rage foolishly convinced them a groundhog can be forced from its burrow by pouring gasoline down the hole followed by a match. As enticing as it may seem, this method of eradication does not work! They found out the hard way it is impossible for a human to outrun exploding gasoline. Experience has taught me the match stems would have to be several feet long to avoid the resulting explosion and flash fire.

I have also been told these very same critters are useful in some northern states in predicting the arrival of spring based on whether or not it sees its own shadow on a specific day. Meteorological science does not support this theory but these are the same folks who wear long black socks with short pants as they pass through our state on their way to Florida. This quirky behavior may help explain why so many of our northern friends are willing to head south as soon as they retire. No person in their right mind would ever retire and move to Detroit.

Be that as it may, as luck would have it, a short time after the deer incident I was speeding along a narrow dirt road in my old pickup and spotted something ahead right in the middle of the road. Coming closer, I realized it was a large groundhog standing upright and probably wondering what was making that strange rumbling noise. Unfortunately, it did not react in time and the impact of my front bumper on his head certainly ended any such thoughts for the moment. Recalling my friend's fondness for groundhog, I prepared to toss the lifeless body into the bed of my truck. My plan was to make my way to his house before rigor mortis set in on what I was certain was a very dead groundhog. Not wishing to get close to very long, sharp teeth, I had wisely placed a rope around the body before swinging the thirty to forty pound critter into the truck bed. My friend was outside when I arrived and was summoned to my truck for the big surprise. And a surprise it was! Up on all fours, the furry critter was looking around and probably pondering how he had gotten into this predicament. His last conscious thought was undoubtedly that of standing in the road and now he was somehow confined to a strange metal box and being stared at by two creatures that experience taught him it was always wise to avoid. It took a lot of effort but I somehow managed to choke back my utter amazement that the groundhog had survived the impact of my truck. Rolling with the flow I casually announced to my friend, "I brought supper." Between the three of us there is little doubt my friend was the most surprised of all. His first question was, "How the (bleep) did you get that rope on him?" It was at that point I realized my friend mistakenly thought that somehow I had managed to run down a very large groundhog and get a rope on it before placing it in my truck. This feat would have put a champion calf roper, not to mention a bulldogger, to shame. As stated earlier, timing is frequently everything to a good story and, needless to say, he never got the full truth of the matter. The last I saw of the unfortunate groundhog was the sight of it being pulled along by the rope around to the dog pen behind my friend's house. It was a matter of pride that my friend had to accept the groundhog, because it would have been rude to refuse such a marvelous gift. Whether the critter wound up on the supper table or was released to continue his destructive ways, I never asked. Sometimes, ignorance is bliss. However, I did notice my friend looked at me in a somewhat different manner from that point on. He had lived a long and interesting life, and Margo and I were blessed to call him and his wife our friends. It was a total joy to sit and listen to his stories. However, it was obvious to me that he had probably never seen anyone rope a live groundhog and had trouble comprehending how that particular feat was accomplished by his much younger friend who was still green behind the ears.

Speaking of furry critters which scurry around on the ground brings to mind a story involving a friend who was an avid hunter of raccoons. First, it is important to remember that the use of the proper name, "raccoon," is frowned upon and use of the shortened version, "coon," is much more acceptable in their presence. Only a total novice would refer to a coon as a raccoon. This might possibly be the only thing coon hunters find offensive, and those who have spent any time in their presence will immediately understand what I mean.

While building our home near the Tennessee state line, I often called upon a fellow by the name of Jimmy to bring his heavy equipment to do some work on our place. He lived right across the state line and generally was able to come to the house rather quickly. As already mentioned, he was an avid coon hunter with the prerequisite pack of hounds whose job it was to tree the coon while the coon hunters lounged around the camp fire and waited for the dogs to strike a trail and subsequently tree the beleaguered coon. Jimmy and I became good friends, and I had many questions about the sport because it was something that had never sparked my interest before meeting Jimmy. Coon hunters relish the entire scenario of the hunt. They certainly enjoy the companionship of being with fellow hunters while sitting around the fire and listening to their hounds in the distance. They can easily distinguish the bark or baying sound of each dog, particularly their own. It has been rumored they often enjoy a nip or two from the bottle. When four coon hunters are present there is always a fifth, if you know what I mean.

While working at the house one day, Jimmy asked if we would allow him and some of his buddies to hunt in the creek bottom surrounding our house. Our land adjoined a large tract of bottom land which stretched about a mile to the state line and was heavily populated by raccoons. We readily gave him permission and the topic had totally slipped my mind until a short time later when I almost shot my friend Jimmy. My wife and I were watching the late news on television right before going to bed when we heard what sounded like a log truck coming up the hill toward out house. Our dog was going into hysterics and couldn't decide whether to protect us or run and hide. Now, we live quite a ways off the beaten path, and folks who come up our driveway late at night are obviously lost or up to no good. It is always much safer to assume the latter until the facts can be straightened out. In such instances, our drill is that Margo goes for the guns while I attempt to figure out what is happening. On this particular night, it was quickly obvious that we were under attack. The truck pulled right up to our carport and at least two men jumped out and headed for the house. My wife screamed, "They're shining lights in the windows, I'm calling 911!" Sure enough, that seemed to be the case as light from what appeared to be flashlights danced across the window glass and onto the floor inside our house. Armed with fully-loaded .38 caliber pistols in each hand, I barged onto the back porch in an attempt to hold them at bay until reinforcements arrived. I was as surprised to see Jimmy standing on my back porch as he was to see me with a pistol pointed at his head. As if it was nothing unusual for him to stare down the barrel of a very large pistol, he said, "We wuz wondering if we could go across your creek bottom. Our dogs have got a big-un treed, and it's a lot easier to git thar from here." Attached to the top of the head of the four hunters was a large cap with a light built into the front. What we thought was flashlights were these head-type lights which freed up both hands for more important tasks. In this case, it could well have been to shoot the cotton-mouths they would probably run across while traipsing across our creek bottom. The beam of light would naturally follow their head as it turned and this was what we mistakenly believed were flashlights shining in our window. Needless to say, it was a while before Margo and I were sleepy enough to go to bed. About an hour later, we heard the report of a single pistol shot in the distance. Jimmy had got his big coon. On that night I learned two more things about coon hunters: they stay up late and they never give up.

There are certain situations in life when neither good luck nor skill dare show their head. One of my favorite singers of all time was a fellow by the name of John Denver. He was very popular in the 1970s and 1980s, until he tragically died in a plane crash in October of 1997. There was a line in one of his songs which went like this, "*Some days are diamond and some days are stone.*" Whether intended or not, those few words of that song contain a world of wisdom, and it would behoove us all to live our lives accordingly. All of us would certainly agree that life is much better when the diamond days outweigh the stone days but, regardless of our situation, all of us experience some of each if we are privileged to live long enough. To put it another way, the sun doesn't shine on the same dog's hiney all day long.

During the early days of my teaching career, I became friends with another teacher whose father-in-law owned several hundred acres of land in Sumter County, Alabama. This was, and still is, a very sparsely populated part of the state located south and somewhat west of Tuscaloosa. It was known then, as it is now, for a large and thriving deer population. Deer hunting in North Alabama was in its infancy at that time, and most deer hunts were not very fruitful because there were few good places for the public to hunt and the deer were few and far between. At least that is the excuse I used.

My friend knew I loved to hunt and graciously made arrangements with his father-in-law for us to come and pick him up in Tuscaloosa on a Friday afternoon, and he would travel with us to his place near Gainesville, Alabama, in Sumter County. It was obvious to me that my friend organized the hunt strictly as a favor for me, because it was easy to tell he was not a serious hunter. This was quite obvious when he showed up wearing highly polished black dress shoes and dress pants for the trip. He also brought along a battery operated television which proved to be as worthless as a side saddle on a hog.

This trip was literally a dream come true for me, because I had always dreamed of hunting in South Alabama. When I was in school in Tuscaloosa, locals told plenty of tall tales of giant deer with huge racks as plentiful as rabbits. However, my life was occupied with far more important priorities at the time and deer hunting was not close to the top of my list. To my way of thinking, this trip would greatly improve the odds for even an incompetent hunter like me.

The day we chose to leave town for the hunt was December 6, 1972. Football fans of Auburn University and the University of Alabama view this particular weekend either with joyous exaltation or deep depression depending on whether you bleed crimson and white or orange and blue. The famous, "Punt, Bama, Punt," game was played in Birmingham at the Iron Bowl on December 7, 1972. There may be one or two people in the state now living who do not know the significance of this game so a little background is probably in order. That year, Alabama was undefeated and ranked second in the nation. A win over their hated rival would put them in a bowl game with a chance to play for another national championship. Auburn was not having a good year and the experts gave them little chance to win. This game and many others since have proven beyond a doubt that most experts are only a legend in their own mind.

Our plan for the weekend was to travel to Tuscaloosa in a borrowed camper, pick up my friend's father-in-law at his home and then travel to his place in Gainesville and hunt until dark. The next morning we would hunt all day and come back to camp and listen to the game on the truck radio. We would hunt most of Sunday before traveling back to North Alabama.

Well-made plans of mice and men frequently go awry and they did on this fateful weekend in more ways than we could ever have imagined. The telling of this story is very painful to me to this very day, and I must cut it short to prevent my tears from ruining my keyboard.

Full disclosure is probably necessary at this point. I have been a fan of the University of Alabama since I was about ten or twelve years old. I lived for football season but followed Alabama teams in every sport that donned a crimson and white uniform. The fact that I had the opportunity to attend this great university did not make me a fan but only enhanced my devotion to the cause. I was a fan long before my feet ever touched the hallowed ground of Tuscaloosa. Perhaps calling myself a mere fan does not adequately describe my situation. The word zealot was closer to the truth then as it is to this very day. Now, on with my story.

Alabama had the game well in hand until late in the fourth quarter when the same Auburn player blocked consecutive Alabama punts and both were returned for a touchdown. Alabama lost the game and consequently an undefeated season and possible national championship. One of my favorite authors, the late Lewis Grizzard, once described an event as, "ripping my heart out and stomping on it." This comes close to describing my feelings about this game, but it is an understatement. I find no reason to dwell on unpleasant matters and will attempt to make my point and move on.

Needless to say, this rather depressing turn of events put a severe crimp in our plans for the weekend and we decided to tuck our tail between our legs and go home that Saturday night. Our camp was quickly broken and we climbed into the truck to head north. To our complete horror and utter dismay, we discovered no one had the keys to the truck. After a lengthy interrogation, one of the hunting party admitted he had the keys in his pocket when all of us went into the woods that morning, but they were now nowhere to be found. Depression hung over our heads like a dark cloud. We had lost the ballgame in the worst way possible and were now stuck in the deep woods of Sumter County as a cold winter night settled around us. Miraculously, the keeper of the keys thought he may have lost them while climbing a tree sometime during the afternoon. He also believed he could find the tree. I had also climbed a tree but had no keys to lose. However, I did have the privilege of observing a huge bobcat as it silently made its ways through the woods. It was a scary but marvelous experience. Unlike my hunting companion, I was absolutely certain a million dollars would not enable me to find that particular tree in the middle of thousands of others. This was a needle-in-the-haystack story if ever one could be conjured up. To put it mildly, my friend trudged into the woods to search for the tree amidst a round of skepticism, and I was the chief skeptic. It was late in the night when we heard him returning and, lo and behold, he was holding the keys aloft like an Olympic torch. Somehow, he had found the tree and crawled around underneath it on all fours turning over every leaf until his persistence was rewarded.

Despite this miraculous turn of events, our departure from Sumter County was not a triumphant one. The path home took us through the city of Tuscaloosa and the campus of the University of Alabama. The entire place resembled London at night during World War II when the German bombers were overhead looking for targets. The entire campus and most of the town was blacked out. There was no doubt the Auburn campus was alive and well on that particular night as Tuscaloosa would have been had the tables been turned.

Perhaps the moral of this story cannot be summed up on a few words. How about, persistence pays off? Or maybe, the grass is not always greener on the other side of the fence, or even in South Alabama. Never underestimate an opponent is surely a gem to be mined from this very sad occurrence. A day can start out as a diamond and turn to a stone or vice-versa in the blink of an eye or the snap of a football. Coach Bryant saw his diamond day turn to stone, and the game haunts Alabama fans to this day. Coach Jordan saw his stone day become a glittering diamond to live on in the annals of Auburn football which is written largely on t-shirts and bumper stickers. Needless to say, the author's day mirrored that of Coach Bryant. Some of the other memorable lyrics of John Denver's song go like this:

Some days are diamond, some days are stone.

Sometimes the hard times won't leave me alone.

Sometimes the cold wind blows a chill in my bones.

Some days are diamond, some days are stone.

John Denver had it right. Regardless, never give up and never listen to experts! Also, hunting in paradise does not automatically make one a good hunter.

Now, back to my own lucky experience which occurred not far from the very road on which the large buck made the fatal mistake of attacking a truck. A year or so earlier, some of my friends and I decided to rent a large tract of land nearby for use as our private hunting club. Tree stands were erected, game plots were planted and we fixed up an old cabin on the place while generously describing it as a lodge. A very nice outhouse was built in the back yard in order to add a touch of civilization of the place. In addition, it greatly increased the odds of being bitten by a spider in the middle of the night, in a very sensitive area I might add. The chance of coming down with hypothermia was always a possibility when trudging outside in the middle of a cold winter night. At best, an outhouse is a dreary place and at night it is even worse. For some strange reason, my hunting companions always found it amusing to engage in sophomoric behavior by bombarding the outhouse with rocks anytime it was in use, and this did nothing to enhance the atmosphere.

The hours to opening day of deer season were counted down much like a kid looking forward to Christmas. On Friday, before the season opened on Saturday, some of my friends took off work and went to the lodge to spend the weekend. They were pumped at the very thought of bringing home a big buck. Having other things to do, I did not go with them. My hunting experience over the years had not been good at all, and I couldn't see it changing anytime soon. Spending long hours in the woods never seemed to improve my luck. I could see myself winning the lottery much sooner than bagging a nice buck. Besides, why sleep in a mice-infested, drafty, old cabin when my own bed was less than thirty minutes from the hunting site? On Sunday after church, my wife and I had a leisurely lunch at a nice restaurant. We went home where I watched some football, took a short nap, and then I decided to drive up to the hunting club and spend a couple of hours just sitting in the woods. Actually, I really do enjoy sitting in the woods and would highly recommend it to those who have never tried it. Besides, my out-of-state hunting license coupled with my club membership fee had cost me a small fortune, and I needed to get some use out of it.

The old cabin on the property was situated in a little creek bottom between two rather steep, heavily wooded hills. A check of the map in the cabin revealed where my buddies were supposed to be. Actually, the only purpose the map served was to tell other hunters where each of the others thought they were going when they left for the woods on their four-wheelers. Guys who spend thousands of dollars on a four-wheel drive, all-terrain vehicle cannot bear the thought of it standing idle for more than fifteen minutes, so the hunting site marked on the map was rarely accurate. Not owning a four wheel drive vehicle, I decided to climb the hill closest to the cabin to avoid venturing into any area already occupied and risk getting shot. Unfortunately, there are some hunters who shoot first and ask questions later, and I wasn't real sure about some of the other guys and their guests. The hill was more of a challenge than anticipated but, after several stops to put out the fire in my lungs, I finally reached the summit. The beauty and serenity of the woods on a fall day is almost indescribable. Devoid of all man-made sounds, the woods create a sound all its own. The wind makes an audible sigh in the tree tops, the birds are calling out, and the squirrels bark and scamper across the dead leaves. To just sit and absorb the serenity of the scene is relaxing and quieting to the nerves. At this point, the hunting becomes almost irrelevant, and most hunters will admit this to be true.

At the top of the hill, a large oak tree had been blown down in years past and provided perfect concealment. Walking up the trunk about eight feet above the ground, I sat and leaned against a large branch. If not for all the deer moving around, I could have taken a nap. No more than five minutes after I sat down, a doe glided silently past my post. She nibbled around for a few minutes and finally ambled down the other side of the hill, totally unaware of my presence. A few minutes later, another doe crossed the trail in the distance. Then it all broke loose. A sudden, loud rustling noise caught my attention. About 100 feet from me, a buck and three does came thundering out of the woods and stopped in the middle of an old logging road. The buck, a nice six-pointer, was more interested in the does than he was in checking out the area for danger. That should be a lesson to all men: look before you leap. Females of most all species will probably be around forever but your life is a one-time thing.

Since I was supposed to be deer hunting, I decided to take a shot. My marksmanship has always been suspect and it was no different this time. The sound of my rifle shot was probably muffled by the trees and the small bunch of deer initially seemed confused before running directly away from my position in the toppled tree. For some strange reason, at this point the buck did something very dumb, and he paid dearly for his mistake. Before I could relax, the buck, apparently unable to pinpoint the source of the noise, came bounding back down the trail directly toward me. This time he stopped just a few feet away. My next shot was a good one, but it did not bring the buck down immediately. Obviously wounded, he disappeared over the side of the hill I had just ascended. Waiting a few minutes, I climbed down from the tree and found a blood trail in the leaves. About halfway down the hill, I spotted him on the ground. As luck would have it, he had collapsed just a few feet from the side of the cabin. This was definitely a case where the blind squirrel finally found an acorn.

My next step, after making certain he was dead, was to drag him to the pulley we had attached to a nearby tree. Knowing I would work up a sweat, I first removed my camouflage coveralls and put them in my truck. This left me wearing a t-shirt and blue jeans standing beside a six point buck almost on the back porch of the cabin. This is the sight my friends saw as they began to emerge from the nearby woods. They were tired and disgusted after a two day hunt with no success, not even a shot at a deer. Jumping to the wrong conclusion, they immediately misinterpreted the situation and decided I had bagged the deer where I stood. The injustice of the situation was evident on their faces. In spite of all their expensive gear and two days in the woods, they had nothing to show for it. In the meantime, I had apparently taken a nice buck while standing virtually on the back porch of the cabin wearing jeans and a t-shirt. Justice does not always prevail, and luck comes into play in places other than in front of a slot machine.

An explanation on my part seemed to be the right and fair thing to do to help clarify the situation and alleviate their suffering. On the other hand, the fair only comes around once a year, and the fair had come and gone long before hunting season opened. Besides, it would make a much better story if they were allowed to believe what they thought they were seeing. After all, they saw what they saw. The true story was so incredible they would never have believed it anyway. That is the way the tale would be told at work the next morning and forever after.

My very good friend, Eddie, loved to relate a hunting tale of his own even though it had nothing to do with deer or other wild game. Eddie had a house full of children and was responsible for several other members of his extended family under his roof. As with many school teachers, he had to go to extra lengths to make ends meet. They raised a large garden and he was an avid do-it-yourselfer out of necessity. Eddie and his family lived in a very pleasant two story house on a hill above a small creek. His place consisted of several acres on the hill behind the house and dropped off into the creek bottom. While not big in the cattle business, he did run a few head mainly to help supplement the dinner table. As with most of his other chores around the house, his entire family was involved when it came time to slaughter and butcher a cow. Most folks who slaughter their own cows, pigs, chickens, or whatever, more than likely select the critter that is causing the most problem at the time. Among every bunch of cattle, there is always one who is a nuisance. One of them will always cause the others to run away at exactly the wrong time, to get out of the pasture, or bully the rest of the herd. On this particular occasion, Eddie had selected a bald-faced black cow which was always knocking the other cows away from the feed trough. He would make preparations to hang the cow from a tree limb after shooting it and dragging it to a small shed which had been used to house dairy cows long ago. There, the entire family would butcher and wrap the meat for the freezer.

With one of his sons accompanying him, the pair trekked through the creek bottom looking for the small herd of cattle. It didn't take long to spot them. Eddie quickly shouldered his rifle and fired at the one selected to grace the dinner table for the next several months. Many years earlier, I had accompanied him on one of his cattle hunts and witnessed him make a remarkable shot to bring down a cow running at full speed. But, as will sometimes happen, on this occasion he hit the cow but failed to kill it. She continued with the others and disappeared into the trees and then the entire herd ran up the side of the hill. He told his son to circle around and make his way to the top and try to drive the cow back toward him. In the meantime, he continued in the direction of the fleeing bunch of cows. About halfway up the hill, he spotted what he thought was the wounded cow and immediately dropped her where she was standing. Making his way to the fallen animal, his son soon joined him after hearing the gun shot.

Sort of bragging, he said to his son, "Got her with one shot. What do you think about that?"

His son replied, "Why did you shoot that cow, Daddy? The one you shot the first time is dead at the top of the hill."

The chore of butchering one large cow is plenty of work, but with two on the ground the family worked late into the night. One thing was for certain, they had a lot of beef for the table for a good while, not to mention a family tale which would last for generations.

When the next hunting season rolled around, for some reason I had no desire to hunt. Despite living in an area with an abundance of deer and turkey, the interest was just not there any longer. Maybe it was the early morning cold, sitting in a tree stand for hours at a time, painful joints after climbing through the steep hills and hollows, or something undefinable like getting older, I just quit cold-turkey.

With my track record, hunting for sport makes more sense than hunting to put food on the table. Hunger would be my constant companion if the frequency of my meals was dictated by my hunting skill. So, hats off to all those hardy souls who sally forth on bitterly cold mornings to sit in tree stands or ground blinds. Keep up the good fight and be safe! Don't forget to call your wife as often as possible.

******

Jackie Hastings

The Man with One Arm

The school secretary's desk was only a few feet away from the side door to my office. It was almost impossible not to overhear the conversations from the main office when the door was open. I was nearing the end of a very unhappy year serving as the assistant principal of Appleby Junior High School. I began my career in education teaching science to seventh and eighth graders at this school, and it was, without doubt, the best school of its kind in the state. The old building was constructed in the early 1900s and eventually gave way to the wrecking ball. The physical structure left a lot to be desired as far as being set up to utilize what was considered to be new technology at the time, but the teachers and staff worked together to make Appleby a great school. Bats in the attic, radiators hissing in every room, and a library the size of a large broom closet failed to deter the close-knit atmosphere between faculty and students.

An administrative position was not anywhere on my bucket list at the time, but like a lot of male teachers, my exit from the classroom for the higher salary of an administrator was inevitable when the opportunity came along. Unfortunately, the same situation exists today, and many folks who love teaching are lured away from the classroom. Soon, I was able to teach part-time and serve as the first junior high school counselor in the school system.

The school secretary was having a conversation with a man out of my line of sight, but there was just something about his voice that made me think I knew him. Apparently, he was at school that day to pay for a lost book or something of that nature before final report cards were handed out. During those days, grades and most anything else could be withheld for any of a variety of reasons, most often unpaid fees. At one point I heard him tell the secretary he wanted his boy to stay in school and get a good education. If this fellow turned out to be who I thought he was, he had certainly come a long way in his thinking about the value of an education.

As usual, the school secretary was handling his situation with the practiced skill of a veteran in the field. Many in the field of education think the person most useful to the operation of a school is the principal. Those who think that are wrong! Multi-tasking was actually invented by school secretaries before anyone knew the meaning of the word. A secretary who has been on the job for any length of time can answer questions which generally baffle a school administrator. The principal could go on an extended world cruise and no one would really know he was missing for several months. Let the secretary go to the restroom for fifteen minutes and the school begins to fall apart. The principal has no idea where the band aids are kept. The principal cannot locate anything without the assistance of his secretary. She can go directly to any list, form, letter, or folder filed in any one of dozens of four-drawer filing cabinets which have accumulated over the time the school has been in operation. She can immediately contact and dispatch the school custodian to clean up and dispose of any mess anywhere in the school in the length of time it would take the principal to scratch his head. If called upon to locate the mop bucket, the principal is clueless. The secretary can replace paper and ink in the copier while talking on the phone and having a cup of coffee. She can calm distraught students and parents while the principal is on the phone in his office talking to his psychiatrist. When my daughter took her first teaching job and asked for my advice, I told her to immediately make friends with the school secretary, the custodians, and the lunch room workers. This trio can help solve the problems that matter. Today, she considers me a wise man.

The longer I listened to the conversation outside my door, the more familiar the man sounded. As inconspicuously as possible, I managed to maneuver my chair around to a convenient file cabinet so that I could view the entire reception area of the office while pretending to look for something. A quick glimpse in their direction confirmed my suspicions. The face would certainly have fit, but when I saw the shirt sleeve on his left arm pinned to his shoulder I knew exactly who he was. The lower part of his left arm was missing from about the elbow.

In elementary school we all called him Buster, which was what he asked his teachers to call him. We never knew if that was his real name and never thought much about it. We certainly knew better than to just walk up and ask him his real name. Survival is very tenuous in elementary school and some questions are best left unasked. His surname is not important, but it could have been one of dozens of similar kids who attended the elementary school in East Florence where my entire family spent many productive and unproductive years.

A school named Brandon had stood on that particular hill for longer than I could remember. During my lifetime, the site wore out three different buildings. Everybody I knew attended Brandon School. All my siblings, my parents, my grandparents, my uncles and aunts, and all my friends spent some time there. They attended for varying lengths of time and were forced to stay longer as the state began to establish a minimum age at which students could legally quit school. The school was built to educate, as much as possible, the children of the cotton mills, warehouses, and railroad workers who pretty much populated the entire area. It was probably a good thing that schools were not concerned with dropout records at that time. That number at Brandon would have been sky high because unskilled jobs were plentiful, and many parents encouraged their children to quit school and take these kinds of jobs.

Buster and I were in the same room in the fifth grade. He would probably not remember me, because older boys in elementary school rarely know the names of younger boys. I was probably around eleven or so and Buster was around fifteen. This was long before schools engaged in what is known as social promotion. In other words, if you didn't make passing grades, you didn't move up. Buster and I sat across the row from each other for an entire school year. I was just one of many who caught and passed him by as he patiently waited until his sixteenth birthday, so he could quit school and go to work in the community. It was not unusual at all for boys at Brandon School to purposely fail enough grades so they could quit and not have to go to the big junior high school downtown. They appeared fearless to us but apparently they feared what faced them if they were promoted to the seventh grade. Buster knew that he and his large brood of siblings spread out in several grades over the school were often the laughingstock of other students, and it would be far worse in the much larger junior high school. Sometimes we prefer to endure a known amount of misery rather than face the unknown.

Buster lived with his family in an area of East Florence everyone called Railroad Hollow. They traveled around the community on a wagon drawn by a pair of mules who always looked like they could use several extra scoops of sweet feed. To describe the critters as being simply skinny is quite an understatement. Combine this with the fact that the family was very clannish and had few friends among the other kids at school, and that made them a prime target for snide remarks and behind-the-back ridicule. Of necessity, any ridicule had to be extremely covert because a big, strong kid like Buster was not averse to laying his big fist upside the head of any smart-mouthed boy foolish enough to make fun of his family. This knowledge impressed me greatly as I was one of the puniest boys in the fifth grade and had no intention of getting on the bad side of Buster, or for that matter, anyone else prone to violence. Any such thoughts would have been suicidal. As a matter of fact, I had reason to believe I was on his good side because he always picked me to be on his team during recess. Invariably, the teachers always selected the two biggest boys in the class to pick teams for whatever activity might be on the agenda for the day. Since Buster was about four years older than the rest of us, he could launch a softball out of the school yard. Playing kickball on Buster's team was a cake walk. A big part of recess was spent searching the woods down the hill for balls Buster had placed in orbit.

Being a member of the opposing team during dodge ball games was particularly dangerous. Buster could throw a dodge ball about like Dizzy Dean could hurl a baseball and a head shot would leave behind blurred vision and ringing ears for the rest of the day. All eyes were glued to Buster as he scanned the field of sissies to pick out his next victim. The scene was akin to that of a chicken hawk picking its next meal from the nervous flock below. It was considered good strategy by members of the opposing team to step in front of a soft rag-arm lob by another kid just to prevent becoming the victim of one of Buster's heat-seeking missile throws. Discretion is sometimes the better part of valor, and that policy can allow one to live another day. It takes a lot of strategy to survive in elementary school where the law of the club and fang rule. Those of us born without a club or a fang were at a distinct disadvantage and soon learned when to choose flight over fight.

Maybe one reason Buster picked me for his team was because we saw each other outside of school on a regular basis. We were not friends, only acquaintances. While my family didn't actually live in Railroad Hollow, we were very close. We lived only a rock-throw away and the rock didn't have to be thrown very far. The place where we lived could easily be called Hard Times Hill, but we didn't know the difference. There was not a street named Easy in East Florence. My paper route took me up Railroad Hollow every day past Buster's house, and we would acknowledge each other with a quick nod when I passed. Thank goodness a real conversation was never a part of our relationship.

It was Buster's oft-avowed intention to quit school as soon as he could do so. Leaving school before he turned sixteen would expose him to the unwanted attention of the dreaded truant officer. He was willing to bide his time until that possibility no longer existed. There was a barrel stave mill in Railroad Hollow across the creek from his house, and he had been promised a job there as soon as he could legally quit school. Back in the 1950s, a veteran teacher could recognize a dropout the first day they walked into the first grade. There was no stigma attached to dropping out of school in those days. It was a way of life. For most of my life, the number of dropouts in my immediate family far outnumbered those who were able to graduate from high school. Boys quit school to get a job and girls quit school to get married. As a matter of fact, there was no way those in charge of the schools would allow a married girl to remain in school and associate with those who were not married. In most cases these folks became productive, tax-paying citizens. Times have sure changed since Buster and I were in the fifth grade.

The notorious stave mill was very familiar to me. It was easily smelled and heard long before visual contact was made. The noise of the giant saw and the smoke from the constantly burning mountain of sawdust left a vivid impression on my young mind. The smell of burning green oak sawdust is very distinctive and, to this very day, I remember the mill when I am around a campfire. If staying in school could keep me out of a place like that, then so be it. Needless to say, Buster's family were not customers on my paper route because they probably didn't have two dimes to rub together, and reading a daily newspaper was not something considered very important in the total scheme of their lives. In fact, there was a great possibility no one in the house could read. There were other proprieties much more pressing. But, this was not an unusual condition in Railroad Hollow and the surrounding community during the 1950s.

None of us knew the date of Buster's birth but we did suspect it had come and gone when he failed to show up at school for several weeks. He was never around when I delivered my papers past his house, and I just figured he had gone to work. The next news we heard came in the form of a rumor after we had started school the next fall as sixth graders. Someone said that Buster had lost part of an arm in an accident at the mill. This was long before the time for governmental agencies such as OSHA, and adequate safety precautions were not a part of most industrial operations at that time. Mostly because of this tragic oversight, there are many folks in the community jokingly referred to as "nub" or "stumpy" or even "peg-leg" for obvious reasons. Political correctness was not a major part of our existence in those days. More often than not, these unfortunate fellows worked at the stave mill, one of the knitting mills in the community, or for the railroad which dominated much of the neighborhood. It was easy to lose a limb or digit when the entire day, generally ten to twelve hours, was spent in close proximity to sharp blades, textile machines which could almost reach out and pull an arm into its incredibly sharp fast moving parts, or boxcars slamming together with incredible force. Several years later, my family moved out of East Florence and I had practically forgotten about Buster until the day he showed up at school. Actually, I did think about him when I made the rare trip through what was left of Railroad Hollow but all the old ramshackle houses were long gone.

Long forgotten memories can suddenly be retrieved by a variety of stimuli. Sight, sound, or smell can bring back events which have lain dormant in the recesses of our brain for a lifetime. The quick glimpse of Buster's shirt sleeve penned to his shoulder reminded me of the last time our paths had crossed. I was in the final days of my career as a paper boy. Buster's house was the last one I passed in Railroad Hollow before moving into the housing project called Cherry Hill Homes. The two neighborhoods were separated by a short stretch of trees as the hollow gradually faded away and the road ascended to the top of Cherry Hill. The housing project was a pretty rough place and one could easily be set upon by some of the guys my age and older. They might pick a fight just for the fun of it or to take something they wanted, like money. On this day I had just finished my Friday collections, which had to be turned over to the paper on Monday to pay for the papers we had delivered that week. I had a little less than ten dollars in my pocket. Normally, my older brother, Johnny, would have been with me and there would not have been a problem. On this day, I had delivered and collected for both of us. Leaving the project, my normal left hand turn carried me up Colorado Street, and then my home was only a couple of blocks away. To the right I would have returned to Railroad Hollow and the route back home was longer. Before starting up the hill, I noticed three of the older boys just loitering around, and I suspected they were waiting for me and my pocket full of coins and bills. They had given me trouble on more than one occasion. Not being at the top of the food chain in these type situations, I resorted to my favorite weapon. Turning right, I ran as fast as I could back into the hollow. My normal foot speed was comparable to that of a three-toed sloth, and on this day I was further hindered by an empty canvas paper bag flopping at my side and two pockets of the paper company's money. The three came off the hill like a swarm of yellow jackets and immediately gave chase. Buster was in his front yard as I passed, and his empty shirt sleeve was doubled back and pinned at the shoulder. He had plenty of street smarts, and it didn't take him long to figure out exactly what was happening. A quick glimpse over my shoulder revealed he had walked into the middle of the road and stood facing my pursuers. What transpired at that point was none of my business. All I knew was that the chase was over and a safe sanctuary at home was just ahead.

Buster's boy was in the eighth grade and about ready to enter the ninth the day he came by school. I knew his son as I knew most of the students. My job involved school discipline and attendance, and most of my time was taken up with problems involving a reasonably small percentage of students. The boy was never in my office for those reasons and that was a good thing. I did not know him well but I knew him by sight.

It was not particularly difficult to keep up with the boy after he moved on to the high school just down the street. This was something I always did just to keep a record of our former students and how they fared in high school. My counselor friend at the high school may have thought my yearly inquiries about the boy were somewhat unusual, but she was always helpful in answering my questions. During the 1970s, it was a normal practice for the local newspaper to print a list of residents who had joined the military, and soon after graduation I saw the name of Buster's boy among those high school graduates enlisting in the United States Marines. As far as I could determine, he totally disappeared from my radar. Like many high school graduates in the 1970s, he could well have spent his senior trip in Vietnam.

Somewhere along the road between the day Buster left Brandon School for greener pastures and the day he reappeared outside my office, he had experienced an epiphany of major proportions. His attitude toward the value of an education was as different as night and day. Life has a tendency to do that to us in a lot of ways. Beliefs that were once the wellspring of everything we stood for often dry up and disappear like flowers in the winter. Whether it is an event or a process is probably situational. It is a characteristic of most parents to want their children to have more out of their life than they have had during their own lives. It would be a mighty poor parent who didn't try to make this happen, but I know for a fact these type people do exist. My own parents told me many times they wished a brighter future for me. Like many teenagers, I was guilty of taking education for granted and frittered away opportunity after opportunity to better myself while it was there simply for the taking. Squandering a birthright was not invented by my family or generation and it, seemingly, never stops. Hopefully, I came to my senses before it was too late, but maybe I am not the best judge of that situation.

Today, it seems that society is prone to judge people by where they wind up in life as a barometer of their success, or lack of it. Certainly, that would work in most situations. However, there are other instances where the final stop might be somewhat deceiving. A person could wind up as the chairman of the board of a major corporation and be lauded and honored by the elite of our nation for achieving much during their lifetime. That is mighty tall cotton for anybody and not to be taken lightly. Still, if we learn that person was the child of the richest man in America and born with the proverbial silver spoon, some of the glitter might be lost on the achievement because the distance traveled was not very great.

On the other hand, the son of a boy who was born and raised on a hillside in Railroad Hollow, whose outlook was very bleak at best could, in reality, have journeyed miles and miles and very few people would have ever known the magnitude of that achievement. This country is populated by these very folks.

I heard Buster tell the secretary he would have to go home and get the money owed to the school. After he left, I asked the amount and was told it was less than five dollars. I paid the bill and told the secretary to explain it was an error and actually owed by another student with a similar name. As I said earlier, school secretaries can perform miracles and it happens on a regular basis. They also know when not to ask questions. No matter how you figure it, I still came out ahead.

******

Jackie Keating

The Road Home

Sometime during the early 1940s, a fellow by the name of Abraham Maslow developed a psychological theory on the subject of how people prioritize the needs in their life. He theorized such things as food, water, clothing, and shelter as the most basic for survival and thus listed them at the bottom and worked up from that point with the general subject of morality at the very top. In other words, it is fairly certain most folks would secure a food source before they took piano lessons. The list eventually took the shape of a pyramid with a very broad base ascending upward. Surprisingly, his theory was called, Maslow's Hierarchy of Needs. There is no doubt that college students today are studying the same sort of theory. Like most college students, many of the things taught in the classroom seemed to have very little to do with reality. After the exam is over, they are quickly forgotten.

In my own life, I believe somewhere near the broad bottom of very basic needs, I would have inserted something loosely titled, "rest for the soul." Maybe Dr. Maslow meant for this subject to be included in the "morality" section at the top of the pyramid, but if so, it was sorely misplaced. Looking back on my own life, obtaining rest for my soul much earlier would have eliminated most of the angst and uncertainty that came along later.

Since my first book was published, many people have approached me and told me that writing a book was something they had always wanted to do but for some reason or another just never got around to it. The one thing most have in common is that they have a story and really planned to tell it before it became too late. Most of what they wanted to write about had to do with telling about their own life with their struggles and successes. This may not be a universal truth, but it appears to be much more common than I would have originally believed.

So, if it is true that each of us has a story to tell, we must share it before it is too late. It may be the only opportunity we will ever have. If we don't tell our own story, then who will? It is fruitless to worry about those in the past and the way they told their story or failed to tell it. We cannot control how those in the future will choose to tell their story or if they will tell it at all.

It is clear to me that those of us who have obtained "rest for the soul" through salvation have a responsibility to tell our story. Now is our time and the Bible makes it abundantly clear we are to tell others of the amazing grace of Jesus Christ. We hear many voices in our lives. The world calls out to us in so many ways with so many different and alluring utterances that it is easy to become confused. Over the years I have called chickens, pigs, goats, horses, and cows, and they come to me because they know my voice. They know I have something for them. That is the reason it is important to share the message of hope and freedom Jesus offers the world. Those who know Jesus have something of real importance to tell the world: there is rest for the soul in God's Word. If there was ever a time for Christians to share our story, it is now.

One of my favorite stories in the Bible is found in the book of Luke. Jesus had been crucified and the Resurrection had already taken place. His followers had scattered and fled when he was arrested, fearing the same thing would happen to them if they hung around much longer. A fellow who was obviously my namesake, often dubbed "Doubting Thomas," was one of the followers who took flight and ran away from an earlier oath to follow the One they believed to be the long-awaited Christ. Even though Jesus had told them many times He would have to die in order to defeat death, none of them understood.

Two of His extremely discouraged followers were walking the ten or so miles from Jerusalem to the little village of Emmaus discussing the tumultuous events of the previous days culminating, in their minds, in the death of Jesus and the end of His ministry. These two fellows had believed Jesus was the One who would rescue them from the Roman occupation of their country. They, like many others, had mistakenly believed the Messiah would be a military conqueror and rule by the force of armed might. When they saw Him beaten, spat upon, and then hung from a cross, their dreams of deliverance died along with Him. They mistakenly thought it was all over, but in reality, it was just beginning. Seemingly, from out of nowhere, a stranger appeared and began to walk with them as they continued to talk. The two men were astonished that this man coming from Jerusalem apparently had no clue about the events of which they were speaking. When they reached their destination, the two travelers convinced Him to stop and spend the night because He had been such an enjoyable companion and a good listener. As He broke bread with them they suddenly realized all this time they had been talking to Jesus, the Resurrected Christ. The Bible describes it as, "suddenly their eyes were opened."

Sometimes our "eyes are opened" and we instantly know and see the truth. In other cases it may take a lifetime for this to occur. The most important thing to keep in mind is to make sure it doesn't take one second longer than our allotted time on this planet. There is no such thing as a lifetime plus one more second. Sadly, it is possible to keep our eyes so firmly closed that they are never opened to the real truth.

I suppose one of the reasons I like the Emmaus story is

that it reminds me of the many times in my life I have walked with Christ and been totally unaware of his presence. God has promised us we will never walk alone. He will always be at our side. He spoke in spectacular fashion to Moses in the form of a burning bush and His presence was obvious. On the other hand, He walked alongside two fellows on the road to Emmaus and they didn't know it. Many would have us believe that God is dead and no longer speaks to us. I do not believe that for a second! He speaks, but do we recognize his voice?

Just as the two men on their way to Emmaus, I have also tried to put some distance between myself and the pain of facing what I thought was my own spiritual death. Much of my life has been a marathon in an attempt to run away from Christ. The part I got wrong was the fact that Christ defeated death, and when He did so it became possible for people like me to do the same. The Bible tells us that a spiritual death is far worse than a mere physical death. Christ allows us to freely make the decision to conquer death by following Him, but this decision must be made while we are still alive. Once we are in the grave, there is no longer an opportunity for our "eyes to be opened."

As a child, for some reason, I thought I might die during the night and go to Hell. This was a terrifying thought for one so young whose entire world was made up of doing right or doing wrong in the eyes of the adults around me. I was certainly no theologian then, nor have I ever been, but I knew, even in my childish heart, that things weren't right in my life, nor would they ever be until I made my own personal peace with my Savior. It is for this reason I believe Dr. Maslow left out a very import-ant basic need of mankind. Finding rest for our soul is the very essence of life. That took a long, long time for me to realize and is still a work in progress. God is making something out of me and the finished product will be a million times better than the person I was becoming by allowing Satan to control my life. I have heard many people say that they are not what they ought to be but, thank goodness, they are not what they used to be. This is a truth which applies to many of us. But, it is not over yet!

Not long ago, I found a Gideon's Bible which was traditionally given in elementary school to students in the fifth grade. Our politically correct world today has virtually eliminated this practice, which provided many students with the only Bible they had ever seen. As I thumbed through this little book, a flood of memories came rushing back to my mind. Every ten verses or so there were little tic marks in pen or pencil denoting where I left off one night and would read the next ten verses the next night and leave another mark. It takes quite a long time to read the entire Bible about ten verses at a time. If we are to believe what we read on the internet the Bible contains 31,273 verses. Using elementary math, that means it took me about 3127 days to accomplish this task reading about ten verses at a time. This comes out to about eight years, more or less. Basically, from elementary school through high school I stuck with it. My perseverance might be noteworthy but my reasoning was flawed. I had no idea what I was reading or what it meant or the relevance it might have to my life. I just thought that by reading these few verses God might be impressed enough to allow me to get into Heaven. To me, eternity was a matter of a whole bunch of "do's and don'ts". Reading the Bible was obviously on the "do" list. Trying to score points with the Lord was pretty much my method of operation, and it continued for many, many years.

As a teenager I was baptized and joined a church with the hope this would be the event which would assure my entry into Heaven when my time on earth was done. This would have normally been the case except for one critically important factor: it made no difference in the way I lived my life. To me, salvation was an event which took place, and I failed to view it as the life long journey it really is. Apparently, my entire spiritual future was based on the hope that Jesus would come again on a Sunday morning and find me in church. Even better, maybe He would find me in church reading the Bible. Woe unto me if He had returned Monday through Saturday or even after church on Sunday. Later in my life I realized that going to church, much like reading ten verses of the Bible every night, never saved anybody. If my name had been on the membership roll of every church of every denomination in the county it would not have made one bit of difference where I spent eternity. Sitting in a church does not make a person a Christian any more than sitting in a garage makes somebody a car or sitting in a tree makes one a bird. Reading the Bible is a great thing to do, but if it fails to make a difference in the way a person leads their life then it has been for naught as far as salvation is concerned. We may have the Bible memorized and be capable of reciting it verse for verse, but that is not the source of our salvation. The truth of the matter was that if I had been arrested and charged with being a Christian there would not have been enough real evidence to convict me. My life had not changed one iota but I was still trying to accumulate enough quality points to punch my ticket. I mistakenly believed that being a good person would be sufficient, but I was wrong.

There is certainly a lot to be said about being good but the Bible plainly teaches that Jesus Christ is the only answer. The fact is that we can never be good enough to warrant the salvation God freely offers us. If our goodness determined where we spend eternity, what level of goodness would be acceptable to gain us admittance into eternal life? I know I would have opted for the least amount possible. The Bible clearly teaches that salvation through grace is not something we can earn, but a gift from God. Since it is a free gift, we cannot boast about how wonderful we have been to deserve it. If we try to take hold of salvation with nothing but good works, we will come to the conclusion we have earned the right to pass through those pearly gates, but this is clearly wrong-headed thinking. Can you imagine a Heaven where all the inhabitants just sit around bragging about the good things they did in their earthly life? We must accept God's offer of grace for the gift that it really is and believe with the right spirit. It is sort of like someone offering a hundred dollar bill to a beggar. All the beggar has to do is reach out and take it. It is a gift totally unearned by anything we might do.

The unexplainable love God has for us has always been a mystery to me. It has been difficult to believe that God really does love me. All of us know full well the dark secrets we carry with us and believe, since God also knows, we are not worthy of being loved. I think the longer we live for the world separated from God, the more we wonder how we could ever be accepted by God. This is not an unreasonable question but this is where God's unending grace enters the picture. Grace can be viewed as sort of the eraser which blots out all the reasons we believe we are not acceptable to God. I fear many people feel the same way about their own lives and, as a result, believe they are too far gone to be salvaged. There is no life that is so messed up that the saving grace of Jesus Christ cannot redeem and make it whole again. Sadly, we mistakenly believe we must get our life in order and then go to God. The reverse is true. We must go to God first and then our life will get itself in order as we seek to do His will. Thankfully, Jesus didn't come to save the saints, he came to save sinners like me and this knowledge has made all the difference in the world in my life.

Back in the 1960s, when I first started teaching, old style chalkboards were still in use. There is only so much stuff one can write on a chalkboard before it must be erased. Occasionally, with a cloth and a bucket of water, the board was washed and became clean once again and was ready for a new message. This is the way God planned salvation. Once we accept Christ, our old sins are erased and our lives are made clean by the simple act of accepting His Son as our Savior.

The sacrifice Jesus made on the cross stands between our sins and God. Maybe because I rarely went to church as a child I missed this very important lesson from the Bible. A series of wonderful pastors at our church who constantly talked about God's amazing grace caused me to begin to re-think this wrong-headed belief. Once this truth managed to get through my thick head, it was the most amazing thing I had ever heard of and it was there all the time. It is a perfect example of something that is too good to be true.

As an adult I have often fallen prey to the greatest trick Satan has even perpetuated on the world. If we listen to the world long enough, Satan will soon convince us he does not exist. This is accomplished in so many ways they are impossible to count. One of the most obvious is that many churches today seem to be afraid to talk about Satan and the very real presence of evil all around us. Failure to even talk about the devil may convince some that he really does not exist. Sin has become acceptable, and today many things have slowly crept into our life. In fact, we no longer look upon them as being contrary to God's word. Sure, it is much easier to deny the existence of evil and what the evil one has done in our lives. The world would have us believe there are no consequences to knowingly living in sin since everybody else does it.   As long as Satan has us believing his lies, we are right where he wants us to be, even if we are sitting in a church.

During my life I have tried living without God and I have tried living with God. Without a shadow of doubt, living with God is far superior to anything else we will ever find in this world. As a matter of fact, that is the only way we will ever get out of this world alive. I am far from perfect and I recognize that fact every day of my life. One unassailable reality remains perfectly clear: while we trod the face of this earth, none of us will ever be saints. The best we can hope for is to be a sinner who keeps on trying. Once we accept the fact that we are unworthy, but loved, the concept of grace begins to make some sense. All I can do is be thankful that God chose to reach down in a lost world and give me the opportunity to join Him when my days are done on this earth.

When I accepted Christ as my Savior, my worldly problems did not disappear. If my memory serves me right, Satan was sitting on the edge of my bed when I woke up the morning after I was baptized. He was afraid he had lost me and wanted to make sure I knew that God could never love somebody like me. There are still times when I let pride back into my life, but pride is just another of Satan's tricks. If we live with sin long enough we come to enjoy it, and if we are not careful, it will creep back into our thoughts and all Satan needs is a foot in the door. He is kind of like a hog rooting around the edge of a fence. Once he gets his nose under the wire, his whole body follows the nose, and pretty soon he is off and running. I still have thoughts which are far from pure, and probably my biggest sin is failing to pass on the love of Christ to others as Jesus said we should.

Everything our Savior stood for basically told me to replace condemnation with love and, left to its own devices, this world does exactly the opposite. Jesus teaches us that darkness cannot drive out darkness. Only light can drive out darkness and He is the light of the world. As far as I am concerned, we are all in the same boat which is without sails or a paddle on a very turbulent sea. Without the hope given us by Jesus Christ, this little boat is sinking fast in a sea of sin which is what this world has become. We should all be like the hungry beggar who found some bread and went around telling all other hungry beggars where the bread could be found by anyone who took the time to look.

The book, Pilgrim's Progress, has been required reading in most college literature classes for many, many years. It was written by John Bunyan and published in 1678, having been around long enough to make students miserable for a really long time. The main character, Christian, or Everyman, is on the inevitable journey from the world he lives in to the world which is to come. Along the way, he meets a variety of people and obstacles, some which help and others which hinder his progress. Some of those he meets along the way go by such names as Evangelist, Obstinate, Worldly Wiseman, Flatterer, Pliable, Talkative, Hopeful, Ignorance, and many more. He encounters such obstacles as the Slough of Despond, Carnal Policy, and the Valley of Humiliation. The funny thing is that at the time I was forced to read this book I had no clue what it was talking about. Now, many years later, I realize I have met many of these very people and, in fact, could have been their identical twin at various times in my life. I have visited many of the exact same places as I have made my trek from this world to the next and encountered the exact same temptations and obstacles. We often have to take a lot of dead ends before we find the road which leads home.

All of us are now somewhere along this same pilgrimage. This is true whether we believe it or not. Every man, woman, and child ever born into this world will have to make this trip. It is not optional and cannot be avoided. Throughout this trek many decisions will have to be made. The one decision of lasting consequence is whether or not we will allow Christ to walk with us through this life. We can choose life over death and this choice appears to be a no-brainer. The mistake I made for a long time was trying to apply logic to this choice. There is no logic to walking on water, raising the dead, healing the sick, or giving sight to the blind. There is no logic involved in loving me enough to go to the cross for me when I was an unlovable person. There is certainly no logic in walking out of the grave and conquering death for those who follow Him. Sure, there are plenty of unanswered questions about the Bible and why things happen the way they do in this world. But remember, we live in a broken world and God has given us the freedom to make our own decisions. If Satan can convince us to wait long enough to get all our questions answered then he has us hook, line, and sinker. This is definitely a case where time is not on our side. All we have to do for Satan to win is to wait one second too long.

There is a story of three apprentice devils who are being interviewed by Satan. Very shortly the three will be turned loose in the world and the head devil is interested in how each is planning to go about his business of destroying lives. One says, "I will tell them there is no God." Satan responds by saying that won't work because all they have to do is look around and they will know there is a God. The second young devil says, "I will tell them there is no hell." Again Satan shook his head and said, "That won't work either. Many people have lived through hell on earth and they know all about hell." The third apprentice devil proudly looks at Satan and says, "I will tell them there is no hurry." "Wonderful," says Satan, "that will destroy them by the millions."

One day it occurred to me that maybe I should worry about the questions for which I knew the answer rather than let my life go down the drain waiting for answers which will never come, at least in this world. Like many others, my mistake was in believing I should wait until I could get it all figured out and then get my life in order.

I made many wrong decisions along this path but the right one that really mattered was to allow Christ to take control of my life as much as my human condition will allow. Without Him, my life is meaningless and I just drift around bumping into things along the way with no real direction. There are still times when I find myself trying to take the controls back. I have found this is a commitment I have to make every day of my life. On my good days, I do not even make it past breakfast before I have done, said or thought something for which I need another dose of grace. It is not a decision to make just one time and then forget about it. A favorite old hymn is entitled, "I Need Thee Every Hour." The words of this old song have brought comfort to people for many years. Yet, I would take it even further. I not only need God every hour, I need Him every second of every minute of every hour of every day of my life. If we attempt to swim across a wide lake and stop in the middle because we are wrongly convinced we have arrived at our destination, we will undoubtedly drown. Sometimes we allow Satan to deceive us into believing we have arrived and we no longer need God. This decision leads to a fate far worse than mere physical drowning. The walk with Christ, like all other journeys, begins with the first step and that is the hardest one to take. When that first step is taken, the chains fall away and Satan loses!

There is another walk all of us will take during our life and this is probably the most frightening walk of all. One of the most quoted verses in the entire Bible is the twenty-third chapter of Psalms. As a boy in elementary school, our teacher made us memorize this entire chapter and, like most children, it meant nothing to me. It was just another meaningless and painful ordeal associated with school. In this beautiful chapter, we are given the promise that God will walk with us "through the valley of the shadow of death." If there is ever a place where we need a higher power to walk with us, this is it. The fear of dying that was very real to me as a child is replaced with a peace far beyond logic by these few beautiful words.

There is one thing of which I am absolutely sure. If we fail to have our eyes opened by making the equivalent of an Emmaus type walk with Jesus during our time in this life, then the short walk we will all make through that dark valley into the beyond will be all by ourselves. Being alone and staring eternity in the face is the most terrifying experience we could ever imagine. The good news is that it is totally preventable.

It is for this very reason that my walk with Jesus has been the most meaningful experience of my life. It has been far from perfect and I have fallen many, many times. But, in so many words, the Bible teaches us to never, ever, ever give up!

******

Promises to Keep

Each time I entered the nursing home to visit my oldest brother, something inside me seemed to die a little more. My memory of him as a robust man with a laugh that couldn't help but make everyone who heard it smile faded a little when I sat beside his bed. The Parkinson's disease had slowly robbed him of the ability to move and made his voice barely audible when he spoke. Visiting nursing homes and hospitals to watch my father and one of my brothers slowly waste away had turned each visit into an ordeal which made me feel guilty at my own good health and well-being. When I thought about skipping a visit, my daddy's admonition kept popping into my head. On more than one occasion he reminded me that as the youngest of seven siblings, it would be my responsibility to help each of them anytime they needed help. There is no doubt he told each one of my siblings the same thing over the years.

The importance of family, both close and distant relatives, was not to be denied and was very much a part of our upbringing. It was drilled into each of us from birth. My brother, Bill, was convinced our close family ties were simply part of our DNA, handed down from our ancestral Scottish clans who banded together for mutual protection in the highlands of Scotland. From my early childhood, I can remember accompanying my parents to the homes of people who were related in some way. We sat for hours while my parents rehashed the old days and discussed other relatives who were totally unknown to me. These same people, and many others, would come to our house to visit and the same stories were told over and over. Our family visited constantly and, sadly, this trait seems to have disappeared from the scene today. One of my greatest regrets is not paying enough attention to those old family stories so they could be re-told to my own children. Being too young to know any better is a mighty poor excuse that these stories are now lost forever. There seemed to be a connection to family, no matter how tenuous, that must be maintained and that sentiment became such a big part of who we were as a family, it sometimes strained our relations with other people. It was generally understood that if you tangled with one McDonald, you put yourself in a position to tangle with the whole brood.

To lose a loved one very suddenly is tragic and devastating. On the other hand, it is maybe more difficult to be forced to stand by and watch a family member slowly and painfully die. It seems to me that a little bit of pain on a daily basis spread out over several years does more damage than a lot of pain in one big dose. Daddy always taught us if something needed to be done, then go ahead and do it. Just standing around twiddling our fingers is no help to anybody. Helplessness, combined with grief, made a mighty big burden to tote around. There is very little one can do standing around the bed of a dying loved one and that made it very difficult.

Bill was the fourth of my brothers to pass away. He was a highly respected member of the community, well known for his exhausting research and contributions to the preservation of the many historical sites and buildings of Northwest Alabama. He was responsible for the placement of dozens of historical markers in Lauderdale, Colbert, and Limestone counties in North Alabama. Not only did he identify the sites, he wrote the script, designed the signs, placed the order, and frequently paid for them out of his pocket. In addition, he physically put the signs in place, informing the casual traveler of a long gone historical happening on that site. Many times he enlisted the help of his two youngest brothers in digging the hole and physically erecting the extremely heavy and unwieldy signs.

My brother's unique style of writing and storytelling brought to life previously unknown accounts of early settlers, Native Americans, veterans of the Revolutionary War, the Civil War, and both World Wars. He was able to help the people of Northwest Alabama connect with their past and pointed out to them much of the colorful history of this area that had surrounded them throughout their lives without their knowledge. His accomplishments as an author and historian brought him many honors over the course of his life. Bill was the first of our family to obtain a college degree. He did so when he returned home from serving in World War II, after entering the Army during his senior year of high school when he was eighteen years old. He enrolled at what is now the University of North Alabama, took advantage of the GI Bill and became a commissioned officer after completing the ROTC program. He entered the service of his country once again and served stateside during the Korean War. After serving on active duty for several years at Fort Bragg, North Carolina, he came home where he served in the Army Reserves. He eventually retired with the rank of full colonel after a total of 38 years on active duty and as a Reserve.

Bill was a lifelong Methodist, having been heavily influence by the staunch Methodism of our maternal grandfather, Leonard Lindsey. His close relationship with our grandfather Lindsey probably played a major role in his decision to serve as a chaplain for his company while in Europe. A natural transition from that role in the military led him into the ministry later on as a civilian. He loved to tell how he actually became a local church pastor, and it was certainly not according to the normal process of his beloved Methodist church. In an interview a few years before his death, my brother explained how he became a Methodist minister. In his own words:

When I was in Europe, because we were a small outfit in terms of numbers, we didn't have a chaplain. That concerned me. I had grown up in the St. James Methodist Church. I loved the sound of those bells on Sunday morning. On Sunday mornings in Europe, I could hear the distant sound of church bells ringing, calling people to church. Somehow, I had the urge to establish my own church services.

I called a meeting and asked my bugler, whose name was Willis Goldsmith, I said, "Willis, I want you to sound church call Sunday morning."

He said, "But, sir, we don't have a chaplain."

I said, "Well, we're going to have one Sunday morning. So, you sound church call."

He did and we had a good congregation. Later, after the war, he asked me when we were having a reunion, if I had known at the time he was a Jewish bugler if I would have called on him anyway. I said, "I didn't know what you were, but I knew what I wanted."

So, we had the bugler who was a Jewish believer sounding church call. He never did miss any of my services.

We were in a sort of back echelon area. When we had deaths, we had to take the bodies into Paris and turn them over to the Graves Registration and Command. I told a fellow by the name of Pennigan, who was our medic, that the next time we had a detail going into Graves Registration and Command that I wanted to have the honor of taking those deceased soldiers in for burial.

He contacted me and said, "I have three men who are deceased and ready to go if you are." I took over the Army ambulance, drove it to Paris, and reported into Graves Registration and Command. I asked the men who were receiving the corpses if they had a chaplain.

They pointed me to a building three blocks away where there was the office of the chaplain.

I found out later that he was General Eisenhower's personal chaplain. I didn't know it at the time. I told him what I was doing and he was very excited about it. He said, "That's great. Let me help you. How can I help you?"

I said, "If you have hymn books, we don't have a hymnal.

Only thing I have is a Bible."

He said, "That's no sooner said than done." He had his assistant gather up about two boxes filled with hymnals and put them in my ambulance. He said, "Would you need a field organ?"

I said, "Well, I don't have anybody to play a field organ."

He said, "Let me give that to you and you'll find somebody to play it."

So we had a pump field organ. I had a good friend that I had known even before we got to Belgium. He became my organist. I led the singing and did the preaching and we had a good service as you could expect to have in any town anywhere. Not because I was the preacher but it was because of the enthusiasm of those young men who were so glad, as I was, to have a place to worship.

When I came home, I started college.

My wife's grandfather was a retired Methodist preacher.

The people down at Canaan Methodist Church in west Lauderdale County were without a preacher. They asked Brother Hall, my wife's grandfather, if he would come and preach for them.

He said he was not able to make the trip every week, but he had a grandson who preached while he was in Europe and he may be interested in doing that. So, I became the pastor of the Canaan Methodist Church.

When I started preaching at the church, it was on a circuit headed by a preacher by the name of Roberts. We had about thirteen people to be baptized and taken into the church. He found out about it. He looked me up at college and threatened me. He said, "I'm going to bring charges against you. You're preaching in a church that belongs to the Methodist Church and I'm the pastor. You're in violation of the rules and regulations of the Methodist Book of Discipline.

So I went to see the district superintendent at the parsonage. His name was Dr. Dunn. I rang the front door bell and he came to the door. I introduced myself. I told him that I needed to explain what I was doing. He said, "Come on in."

We sat down and he asked me hundreds of questions it seemed: about my faith, my belief in Christ, what I did believe. It must have pleased him because he raised his hand and said, "I hereby appoint you as pastor of the Canaan Methodist Church."

That's how I got started. I stayed with the church in the role of pastor at a number of churches in Lauderdale and Colbert counties. As I look back across the years now, those were the most precious years of my life preaching from the pulpit in those small churches.

I had a wonderful ministry. As the old song goes, "I wouldn't take anything for my journey now." I'm just glad that I had the opportunity to serve the church.

It seems that my brother Bill was caught in a sphere of influence between two staunch Methodist gentlemen. One was his own grandfather, the other, was his wife's grandfather. Some might say he was caught between a rock and a hard place. In my opinion, it was my brother's calling to be a pastor. If not for the two grandfathers, something else would have steered him to the Methodist Church.

However, his journey from the military to the church had one more twist. Here is the rest of the story in his words:

After I finished my college education, the Army called me back into the Korean War. The district superintendent-can't remember his name now-he got all upset when I showed him my orders to return to active duty the following week. He said, "I want you to go to Birmingham right now and talk to the Bishop. Let him contact the Army officials because you're essential."

Well, I didn't think I was essential. I didn't want to play that game, but I went anyway. I sat down in front of the Bishop. I told him the story of what was going on. Instead of calling the Army and trying to get me cleared of any active duty, of being away from my church, he came around and knelt at the side of the desk next to my chair and prayed a long prayer that I've thought about many times.

He said, "Lord, we need this man, but we know that our country needs him too. We want to pray not for our sake but for Your sake, Your kingdom. Take him and bless him and be with him and bring him home safe."

That was my entrance, my transition, from the ministry back into the Army.

He went on to serve as a pastor to many small, rural churches in Lauderdale and Colbert counties and did so for a period of thirty eight years. He did not preach at that many different churches because he stayed at one church 16 years, another one 12 years, and another one 10 years. This fact alone speaks highly of the love and respect his congregation at these churches had for him. Pastors of the United Methodist Church rarely stay in the same church for more than five years. As a child, I remember occasionally going with my parents to hear him preach and their pride in their oldest child was evident. As a matter of fact, the only time either of my parents took me to church was to hear Bill preach. They sat in the pew and beamed like the Pope himself had just handed down a blessing.

In addition to all these jobs, Bill's primary employment was with the Tennessee Valley Authority. He worked for that agency for thirty-seven years where he was the chief of the budget control staff at the National Fertilizer Development Center in Muscle Shoals. He was chairman of the Florence

Historical Board as well as historian for the city of Florence. In addition, my brother was a member of the American Legion, Alabama Historical Preservation, Inc., Kennedy-Douglass Center for the Arts, Sons of the American Revolution, and Clan McDonald USA and Scotland. In 2006, he was granted an honorary Doctor of Humane Letters by the University of North Alabama for historical research and writing that had lasted a lifetime.

Born and raised in the Sweetwater neighborhood of Florence, he was recognized as a Man of the Year at a reunion of former and current citizens of this very unique community. He wrote extensively of Sweetwater and its inhabitants and was able to help keep the legacy of the community alive after it went into a steep decline. In recognition of his body of work over the course of his life to promote the study and continue the rich legacy of the North Alabama area, the Florence-Lauderdale Library established the William Lindsey McDonald Endowment in his honor and memory.

The honors and awards listed above, and I am positive some have been omitted, tell of the many accomplishments of my oldest brother. But they only tell a small part of the tale. These awards undoubtedly represent what others thought Bill McDonald was, but they fall far short of completing the story. They in no way define him as the person he was and do not come close to even beginning to describe the legacy of family, dignity, trust, and leadership he left with the family and friends who knew him. Bill was the glue that held the family together for many years. He was the organizer of family gatherings. He was the one we called when we decided to get married. I tried to pay him five dollars when Margo and I were married, but he refused payment, explaining with a twinkle in his eye that it was partial payment for all the post holes I helped him dig at his place over the years. Bill spoke only good things about the biggest rascals in the family, and, as he told me one day in private, it was a stretch to come up with something good to say about some of our blood kin. He was the bail bondsman for brothers, uncles, and neighbors who frequently ran afoul of the law, generally from over indulging and looking at the sky through the bottom end of a whiskey bottle. He was the marriage counselor, the war veteran, the only college graduate most of us knew, and the one who always felt it was his responsibility to smooth hurt feelings. Bill was the one who always reached out to family members who felt hurt and left out and felt responsible for drawing them back into the family circle. He always said grace at our gatherings and drew a crowd when he began telling stories. Sometimes Bill would get to laughing so hard at one of his own stories he could not continue. His laugh was not superficial but came from deep within his body. Those who never heard Bill McDonald laugh missed a real blessing.

Finally, there was the time when our brother Johnny needed a kidney and most of the family agreed to be tested as a possible donor. Bill and I turned out to be the closest match, and both of us quickly agreed to be the donor. It was basically a no-brainer since Johnny and me were very close in age and grew up together. There was absolutely no doubt in my mind about being a good match. I just knew it and had long ago had the conversation with my wife about donating a kidney.

Late one night, I answered a phone call from our oldest brother. Bill explained that as the senior brother in the family he was pulling rank on me and he would be the one to donate a kidney. His logic was that at his age this would be his last opportunity, and my kidney could be used down the road if and when the first transplant failed. Thankfully, the transplant was a resounding success, and our brother was able to enjoy many more years and get to know six strapping young grandsons who otherwise would have never known their grandfather who loved them more than life itself. I have actually heard of families where someone died because no family member would step up

188 Promises to Keep

and agree to donate a kidney. Sleep must come mighty hard for these folks after the funeral.

There was a distinct difference in the cohesion of our family as Bill grew older and declining health began to play a role in his activities. Our family got together less frequently during his waning years, and it is an understatement to say that we suffered greatly from that loss of leadership.

I had come on this day to report to my oldest brother that the last of the promises made to him at the beginning of his illness had finally been accomplished. Almost a year earlier, he realized his time was short and needed help to get some things done he could not hope to accomplish in his condition. Bill's career in the military apparently caused him to rely heavily on reports, and he insisted on frequent updates on the progress of whatever assignment he had given me. As I have shared this story with others, I have often been asked about the heavy burden he seemingly placed on my shoulders by asking for my help with what turned out to be projects that consumed a great deal of time. Actually, I considered it an honor that he felt his youngest brother could handle such responsibility.

It gave me a great deal of pride in making good on all the promises to my brother, and at the same time, trying to be faithful to my daddy's advice about the importance of family. This was something those without the bonds shared by a large family would never understand.

My mind drifted back to my visit to the assisted living facility much earlier when he told me he had a favor to ask of me. In no particular order, he wanted me to put together some of his writings and finish a book he knew now would be impossible for him to complete as he originally intended. He had written books detailing the McDonald and Lindsey families and had always planned to write about the Johnson side of our mother's family. In addition, he also wanted me to locate and mark the grave of a distant relative who was a Revolutionary War soldier. He had only a vague idea where this gravesite was located, but it was across the state line in Tennessee. As I was to discover later, this particular task would involve little in the way of mental power but a lot in the way of physical exhaustion and perseverance. The third favor he asked of me was to involve a great deal of driving around lonely country roads and asking complete strangers questions, which made them wonder what I might be up to. As a young boy he and some of my other older brothers had helped our daddy build a log cabin in Wayne County, Tennessee. He wanted me to find the cabin and bring him a picture, if it was still standing. It seemed to be very important to him and, consequently, it became important to me. His memory of its location was very vague, and over the years the field and woods roads had become straightened and paved, and the topography had been greatly modified by farming and logging operations. It was not quite as bad as finding the proverbial needle in the haystack but almost.

The journey from a healthy, robust man whose main pleasure in life was researching the historical archives of his community and writing the history of the people and places around him, to his current condition of viewing the world flat on his back in a nursing facility had been a long and painful one. My brother Bill had grown up working around, first our family home, and then his own place. His love of books and research caused many folks to mistakenly categorize him solely as an academic, but in reality, physical labor was a big part of his life. He was no stranger to fence building, plowing, erecting sheds and barns, and remodeling his own home. In spite of this background, he loved to tell the story about the advice our cousin Minnie Rickard gave him when he was growing up. She lived with her husband, Hunter, a short distance up the road from our house. They had a well with an old hand-pump in the yard ,and their house was a favorite destination on hot summer days because of the ice-cold well water. Aunt Minnie was not one to mince words, and Bill said she once told him, "Billy, you better get a good education because you shore can't make a living doing nothing else." Daddy and I spent many Saturdays at his house helping him build barns and fences. This never seemed like hard work to me because it was always a joy to be able to spend time with him. He wore a lot of hats, and his many other responsibilities were very demanding on his time. I suppose that is a common feeling among a lot of younger brothers.

Bill was a veteran of World War II, having arrived in Europe shortly after D-Day and spending the remainder of the war in Belgium during extremely cold weather. Infantrymen have been the backbone of every army ever formed and their role has changed little over the centuries. Braving the elements during the winter and sleeping outside in the extreme cold and snow of a European winter was not something boys from the South relished. It is a historical fact that the United States military did not adequately clothe those soldiers in the field, and many froze to death during the extremely cold winters. As he told me frequently, he came as close to freezing to death in the forests of Belgium as he ever wanted and spent much of the rest of his life trying to keep warm. He was eventually pulled out of the infantry and sent into a situation where he ended up being the Sergeant Major of a prisoner-of-war depot which was home for some 5,000 captured German and Italian soldiers. Later in life, with a day's labor behind him, nothing suited him better than sitting in front of a warm fire on cold winter nights, drinking coffee and telling stories. Sharing just a few of these moments with him has always been a great joy to me.

Bill finally succumbed to his illness on June 20, 2009. Several years earlier he had been diagnosed with Parkinson's disease. At that time Bill and all of my siblings and a few cousins met every Wednesday morning in downtown Florence and had breakfast together. At that point in our lives, we were retired and our weekly get together was something all of us enjoyed. I was told by one of the regular customers at the restaurant that we always seemed to be having so much fun, that he wanted to come over and join us. He never actually joined us, but he did move to the table next to where we always sat. The old fellow's wife had died, and the obvious camaraderie of this boisterous band of brothers and cousins was a joy for him to be around. Usually the early arrivals stood around outside talking until all the others had arrived. Like most members of our family, Bill often arrived early and I watched dozens of times as his little white Ford station wagon slowly made its way down Florence Boulevard and pulled into the parking lot.

As time passed, my brother grew painstakingly cautious in the way he walked and moved, and it was easy to see the effects the disease was having on his body. As the tremors slowly took control of his hands, eating became more difficult. Being the consummate southern gentleman, he always apologized to the waitress for making a mess and did his best to clean up the area around his plate. Eventually, I began to feed him because he was unable to use an eating utensil of any kind. I think he suffered this indignity as the price to pay for continuing to have breakfast with his brothers and cousins. This wonderful time of sharing a meal with my brothers fell by the wayside after Bill entered the nursing home.

My brother is remembered by a lot of people in a lot of different ways. He was a gentleman, a writer, a pastor, a historian, a scholar—and I remember him for all these things. But the thing I most remember about my brother was his sense of humor. He found humor in a lot of things, especially the people around him. However, he kept most of these things to himself until he was around his brothers and he told stories on himself that he would not have dared to repeat in public. One of his favorite stories involved his trip to the doctor as they attempted to diagnose the source of his failing health. Noticing his trembling hands, the doctor asked him if he drank a lot. He replied, "No, I spill most of it." I laughed at that story every time he told it and never tired of watching him laugh at his own misdeeds.

Eventually, he was unable to continue to drive and I began going by his house on Wednesday mornings and taking him to breakfast. Early on, it was simply a matter of waiting outside until he slowly walked to my parked truck. This worked for a while but he eventually graduated from a cane to a walker to keep from falling. Soon, a wheel chair was needed for him to maneuver inside and outside his home. The house he and our daddy had built in the early 1950s and he later had remodeled was a beautiful, comfortable home in a rural setting but totally unfit for a wheel chair. I gladly volunteered to make his inside doors easier to pass through and built a ramp so that his chair could be taken outside more easily.

All of this time, Bill continued to sleep upstairs in his office/ bedroom. It had become increasingly more difficult for him to sit upright in his bed in order to get out of bed at night and in the mornings. We designed a rope and pulley system that enabled him to pull himself into a sitting position with the rope and then stand. He jokingly told me he just had to be careful and not hang himself in the middle of the night. Dozens of times when we arrived back at his house from break-fast he asked me to come inside because he had something he wanted me to see. When I followed him into the house and up the stairs to his office, I marveled at his determination as he slowly and painfully made his way up the steep, narrow stairs with no assistance. The fact that he didn't die from a fall was a miracle in itself.

It eventually became impossible for him to stay at home, and he agreed to move into an assisted living facility. His deter-mination not to be a burden on others was a big factor in this decision. It was here, more than a year before he died that he asked me to help him complete some of the tasks he desperately wanted to bring to fruition. There was no doubt in my mind that he knew his time on earth was short, and there was no way I could have refused his request and continued to live with myself. A popular song from a few years back recorded not only by a group calling themselves the Hollies, but other groups as well, contains a verse which captures perfectly my feelings:

> It's a long, long road
>
> From which there is no return
>
> While we're on the way to there
>
> Why not share
>
> And the load doesn't weigh me down at all
>
> He ain't heavy, he's my brother.

My brother had been writing for many years. Many of his stories had been submitted to daily and weekly newspapers and published for a long period of time. His musings on daily happenings and observations gave him a level of name recognition that was at least equal to his name recognition as a historian and author. Many of his short stories had been collected and published in book form giving him quite a large local audience. As the Parkinson's disease slowly robbed him of the ability to read and write, his articles appeared with decreasing frequency. Many times I was asked by people who knew me or those I had just met if I was related to the author with the same last name. Bill joked that the McDonalds were generally short and in possession of a rather large head which he said was a result of Native American bloodlines from our great, great-grandmother, Higgins, who was a Chickasaw Indian. His assertion that the Chickasaws were frequently referred to as "roundheads" was never proven to my satisfaction, and I accused him of making it up just to justify his big head. My point is that we shared enough of the same physical characteristics for those who saw us side by side to recognize us as brothers.

A humorous incident occurred once when we were both at the same social function and just standing around talking. The local superintendent of education approached and spoke to Bill. The fellow also knew me but he didn't want to acknowledge it. I was the president of the local teachers association, and he considered me nothing but a rabble rouser and a union boss who was prone to bring controversial issues to his quiet, staid board meetings. Bill had such a high reputation as a scholar and gentleman, the superintendent absolutely refused to believe we were brothers, despite the physical resemblance. I was never quite sure whether my boss's opinion of me improved as a result of this startling revelation or his opinion of Bill fell a few notches once he realized we actually were brothers. This became one of my brother's favorite stories and I can still hear his uproarious laughter as he related it to other family members. Bill's wife, Dorothy, once told me I looked so much like him she wanted to slap me. It was my belief at the time that she was only joking, but I was never really sure.

While confined to a bed and wheel chair and away from his office and thousands of historical documents, my brother very much wanted to continue writing, at least for the local newspapers. On a whim, one day I took my tape recorder with me while visiting and told him to put his articles on tape and I would type them up for his inspection and final approval. So we began a system that allowed him to submit many newspaper stories and continue to be published, even though he was physically unable to continue researching and writing out his articles by hand. When he needed to verify something I was dispatched to the local library to look through genealogical records or census information. I have often wondered how much different it would have been had all the computer research tools been available to him during his life. He did all his research the hard way. Libraries, court houses, interviews without the benefit of a tape recorder, census documents, hand written notes, thousands of pages of machine copies of records, all meticulously put together into a document and then corrected time and time again until he felt it was good enough to submit for publication. The genealogical research tools, Google, email, word processors, even cell phones; all these innovations came after the bulk of his work was done. One can only imagine what he would have accomplished had he been able to utilize all the marvelous high tech research, communication, and printing tools available today.

Using our Stone Age method, it generally took several trips to complete one article to his satisfaction. By the time his original words were typed and read to him, he had frequently changed his mind and major changes had to be made. Many times he changed a sentence or paragraph because he didn't like the way it sounded when read back to him or he wasn't 100% sure of the accuracy of the sentence. He absolutely refused to put anything in any of his writings which may not have been factual. This system worked well until he decided to abandon it and concentrate on assembling the material for his final book on the Johnson family. All of his energy came to focus on this one project, and everything else took a back seat.

Thus began my work to fulfill my promise to organize and have published his long intended book on the Johnson side of our family. My first contact was with Angela Broyles, owner of Bluewater Publication Company, located at that time in Killen, Alabama.

Angela and my brother had become acquainted much earlier when she was researching historical documents to assist her children in local history as they were being home schooled. By that time, some of his earlier works were out of print and no longer in circulation, so she offered to reprint many of his earlier books. This arrangement worked out very well and he suggested to me that I contact Angela and tell her what he wanted to do. It was immediately obvious that Bill would not be able to do any more extensive research and absolutely no writing on this project. Fortunately, much of the material for the book was already in my possession in the form of hand written papers on individual family members and a series of letters he had written to our cousin, Judi, as early as the 1970s.

Judi was our uncle Claud's daughter who lived in Montgomery. She knew absolutely nothing of her father's family and had contacted Bill, at the suggestion of her father, in order to get information on her Lindsey roots. Prior to this time, she had absolutely no contact with any of her father's family. Over the years, Bill wrote a series of letters to her and in great detail told our cousin all about her Lindsey and Johnson people. He had compiled these letters and gave me a copy of them as he did with most of the papers he had written. Bill and I agreed that it would make sense to use these letters as the foundation of the book, and I immediately got to work organizing what we already had and having him record information that would fill in any gaps. In addition, I began to gather old photos that would be appropriate for the publication. This work involved a tremendous amount of patience, of which I have little, and a great deal of organizing ability. Fortunately, my wife, Margo, is blessed with both. Without her help, as with most of the other positive events of my life, this project would never have had a successful conclusion. As we struggled with a title for the book, it became quite clear the most obvious title would be, *Judi Letters*. This book was the last of fourteen books written by my brother and, with the help of Angela Broyles, he lived to see it published. I must add that on the day I delivered a finished copy of the book to his bedside, his gratitude moved me to tears, and all the work put into it did not amount to a hill of beans.

During the time we were putting the *Judi Letters* book together, I was able to begin working on another of the promises I had made my brother. All of my life, I had heard our daddy talk about the cabin in Collinwood, Tennessee he had built after the Great Depression. Daddy and my brothers told countless stories of felling the trees, dragging them to the cabin site, shaping them to fit, and then hoisting them into place. This was long before I was born, and I had never even thought that the cabin might still be standing and never was told the exact location except that it was south of Collinwood.

Daddy had been trapped and almost destroyed by the Great Depression and he always believed bad times would come again. The Tennessee Valley region was hit extremely hard and was considered by many to be one of the most depressed regions of the entire country. Dad cautioned all his children never to owe more than we could pay back, and he tried to teach each of us to be as self-sufficient as possible and not have to depend on others. In order to do this, he felt he must move his family out of town to the country where this type of independent life style would be more feasible. While my brothers Bill, Joe and Dan were boys, he and our cousin Frank Rickard, purchased a large tract of land near Collinwood, Tennessee for this purpose. He never wanted his family to face again the near starvation they had already survived. My brother wrote many times of the hardships faced by our family during the Great Depression. His stories of losing the family home and living in two tents for a couple of years are well known in the McDonald family. The humiliation of being kept home from school by our mother because he had no shoes or coat to wear during cold winter weather were memories my brother never forgot. He remembered the times around Christmas when Daddy had been jobless for months and there was no money for any kind of presents for his children. He wrote of Daddy having to buy food on credit with nothing but a promise to repay when a job came along, and the days he spent helping our dad cut firewood to sell were always fresh on his mind. Bill loved to tell the story of being in the Army during basic training. All the other guys were complaining about the food, but he said he had never had so much food in his entire life, especially when he could eat second and third helpings. It was for these reasons and many others like them that Daddy was determined to get his family out of town, and so he bought land in Tennessee in an attempt to fulfill that dream.

Luckily, about the time I began my search for the cabin, I encountered one of our many cousins, Mary Rickard Hughes, at the funeral of another relative. We were talking about Bill, and I mentioned my promise to try to locate the log cabin our daddy and her daddy, Frank Rickard, had built in Wayne County, Tennessee when my brothers were just boys. She knew the cabin well because after Daddy sold his share to Frank, she and her family lived in it for several years while she was a teenager. This was news to me because I had never known she actually lived in the cabin as a girl. She also remembered her father and mine building the cabin and my mother's steadfast determination not to move that far from her family home in Florence. As a matter of fact, she had a painting of the cabin someone had given her years earlier. During our conversation she told many stories of life in a very rural part of the South during very difficult times. Their only source of water was a spring which was at the bottom of a steep hill behind the cabin. Two or three trips a day up and down that hill could "wear a body out" as she told me. The closest school was in Collinwood, Tennessee several miles and a long, lonely bus ride to the north. Her main worry about moving so far out of town, she said, was that as a teenaged girl she was certain there were no boys within miles of her lonely cabin far out in the woods. Much to her surprise, she soon realized there was a boy behind almost every tree and most of them came knocking on her door. Soon, I received in the mail a package with a picture of the painting. Now, I had something concrete to try to find because I knew exactly what it was supposed to look like. However, she was not able to nail down the exact location because of the many years that had passed and also because the land in and around that region had changed so much over time due to logging and farming in the area.

My current home is only a few miles from Collinwood and it was a short drive to the area where I began my search for the cabin. Alone, and sometimes with my wife, over a period of many months, we drove the roads south of Collinwood, looking for something resembling the picture we had of the cabin. We began with the roads immediately south of the city and would drive each road until we were certain we were in the wrong place. Often, we stopped at houses and asked the local residents if they knew of the location of the cabin in the picture. On one occasion, we were stopped by a deputy sheriff inquiring why we were driving so slowly and perusing all the houses. A resident had reported a couple was driving around looking for houses where the occupants were not at home and thought we were burglars. This search continued for about a year and we moved farther and farther south, almost to the Alabama state line. Then it happened; we found the cabin. Turning off the main highway, we had taken a right hand turn when the two lane county road split. We had traveled only a couple of miles when we spotted a rather new, brick house on our right. As we passed the house, my wife looked behind it and, presto, there stood the cabin. It was almost completely obscured by the new house and we could have easily driven right past it. Not knowing what our reception would be, I went to the door and knocked. It was answered by a young lady who was visiting her parents who lived in the house, but they were not at home. After explaining my mission she was very helpful, giving us permission to look at the cabin and take pictures. The only difference was that a shed had been added to one side. Otherwise, it was identical to the picture given to me by our cousin Mary Hughes. I made several return visits, eventually meeting the owner. He was pleased to find out the history of the cabin and informed me he purchased the property sight unseen on the computer. Bill was fascinated when he heard how the current owner had bought the property. He could not comprehend someone buying a place without walking around it and giving it a thorough once-over.

On one trip I took my brother Joe, who had helped built it and my nephew Phillip, whose daddy, my brother Dan, also helped with its construction. Joe immediately recognized the place and walked down the steep hill behind the cabin to the old spring which was their water source. He had mentioned earlier, that he would remember the location of the spring which was located at the foot of the hill which he climbed many times with a bucket of water. When I began my search for the cabin, I asked Joe to write down what he remembered about the cabin. This is what he wrote:

The best I can remember, I was about nine or ten years old when Daddy and Frank Rickard purchased some wooded farm land about six or seven miles south of Collinwood, Tn. It was a good ways off Highway 13, but I do not know exactly how many acres. When it got warm enough, Daddy would take me and Billy and Dan up there to do minor work building the log cabin.

Daddy and Frank and Hunter Rickard (Frank and Hunter were brothers) would cut down the trees to be used for the cabin. They would cut so many trees then would start building the cabin. Mine and Billy's job would be to carry water from the big spring about 400-500 yards down the hill from where the cabin was being built. After laying enough logs, Daddy would put concrete in between the logs. He purchased an old hand-cranked cement mixer to mix the concrete in. Mine and Billy's jobs were to bring the water up from the spring and hand crank the mixer for mixing the concrete and sand. Course me and Billy would take the opportunity when we weren't carrying water or turning the mixer to do some exploring around the farm. I remember once when Daddy, Frank, and Hunter were cutting trees I saw a squirrel go up a small tree to a nest. I told Billy I was going up to get that squirrel. Billy telling me that I had better not, that Daddy would get me as he already instructed me not to be climbing trees. Anyway, I climbed the tree but I couldn't get always up to the nest, so I got high enough to stand on a limb and reach up to the nest. I stuck my hand in the nest and that squirrel almost ate my hand up. I was hollering that he bit me. Daddy hollered back and said, what did you say, not knowing I was up the tree. About that time the squirrel bit me again. I said, "G......D......, he bit me again." About that time Daddy saw me in the tree and told me to get my a.... down from there. I got so far and he had to climb up and help me down. My hand was all cut up from being bitten by the squirrel. Needless to say, I got my a..... whipped. I believe he had to quit work that day to bring me home to doctor my hand. That day I would never forget. The word got around in Sweetwater about me and the squirrel. People would see me and ask if I had been after any more squirrels.

The cabin had four rooms and a front and back porch. There was a kitchen, two bedrooms, and a living room. After the cabin was built Daddy built a table about eight feet long and four feet wide for the kitchen to eat on. There was some old cane chairs to sit on. They put an old wood burning stove in the kitchen and a bed in each room. We had an outhouse for the toilet and got our water from the spring. I remember Daddy and Mother would take us up in the summer a few times to spend the weekend. Other than me and Billy, I believe Dan was about six or seven years old and Bobby was about four or five and Sis was a baby. We had some good times up there. I believe that once Billy and Basil Miler rode a bicycle up there. I'm not sure, Billy may know. Hunter Rickard worked at the Florence Lumber Company. He either retired or quit. Hunter and Minnie Rickard moved up there and we would go up sometimes on the weekend. I believe Charles McDonald went up with us a couple of times. I don't remember how long Hunter and Minnie lived there. At some point Daddy sold his part to Frank Rickard.

Frank was in the army during WWII and after he was discharged he married a Butler woman from Cherry Hill and they moved up there. Mary Rickard Hughes (Frank's daughter and my

source for the picture) can probably remember some of that time.
That's about all I remember as I went into the Navy after that and
almost forgot about it until brother Tommy sent me the picture he
made and it brought back a lot of memories.

Finding the old cabin still intact was a source of great joy
in my family. All of us had heard of it dozens of times from our
daddy and older brothers. The fact that something from the distant past that was a vivid and concrete reminder of our family's
history during some very difficult times had suddenly come to
life was amazing. It was no longer an abstract source of a lot of
stories but was something we could see and touch. It made the
long search worthwhile.

The third promise made to my brother involved a
Revolutionary War soldier, John L. Lindsey, who was distant kin.
He was the son of Captain Samuel Lindsey who lived in South
Carolina and served in that state's militia. Young John served
as an orderly to his father and was in the campaign against the
British during the Battle of Kings Mountain. He actually participated in the fighting, according to family legend. Captain
Lindsey was given land in Tennessee as a reward for his military
service. His son moved to the area around Columbia, Tennessee,
in 1818, to acquire the land given to his father. In 1826, according to census records, he was in Wayne County, Tennessee,
near the Natchez Trace. This county is adjacent to the Alabama
state line and members of his family helped open the area of
northwest Alabama to settlers after treaties with the Cherokee
and Chickasaw Indian Nations. John L. Lindsey built a home
near present day Cypress Inn, Tennessee, very close to what is
now known as the Natchez Trace Parkway. Family legend has
it that the cabin was built of chestnut logs on Cooper Creek in
the Cypress Inn area. My brother Bill obtained this information
from the late Elsie Lindsey Bradfoot, who was the great, great
granddaughter of John L. Lindsey. According to Grace Culver, a
resident of Cypress Inn, John L. Lindsey was buried alongside the

grave of his son, Sylvester Lindsey. She remembered the remains of the ancient cabin from her childhood and also that John's grave had never been marked, but it could be located because it was right beside the clearly marked grave of Sylvester. This was the grave my brother wanted me to track down and mark with an appropriate headstone. He said it was imperative to find Grace Culver before it was too late because she had all the details locked in her head. Locating Grace Culver was no easy task.

The only information Bill was able to give me about finding her was that she lived in a mobile home on Pumping Station Road outside of Cypress Inn. Pumping Station road was the name locals had given to county road 227 because of a large natural gas pumping station situated alongside it. The portion of the road in question ran from Cypress Inn to Chisholm Road, south of Collinwood, Tennessee. That was not much to go on but I did manage to locate the residence, but it was empty. There was no sign of anyone and it looked as if no one had lived there for a long time. People in a small place like Cypress Inn basically know each other, especially the long-time residents. The only person I knew was a fellow by the name of Wright. He raised mules and donkeys and I had actually purchased a donkey from him a few months earlier.

Mr. Wright was a real talker. I had visited with him a few times since the donkey purchase and found out he was born and raised within a few miles of his current home. He served in WWII, sloughing his way across France and built his home near Cypress Inn upon returning from the war. I knew if anyone in the Cypress Inn community knew Ms. Culver, it would be Mr. Wright.

He was on the front porch when I pulled into his yard and seemed genuinely glad to see someone. Not only did he know Grace Culver, but she happened to be a distant cousin and he knew exactly where to find her. She had moved from the mobile home and was living with her elderly mother. Instead of directions, he was eager to go with me and take me to her front door. That turned out to be a good thing. We took so many turns onto narrow dirt roads that I would have never found the house by myself. After traveling several miles off the beaten path, we pulled into the front yard of a pleasant country home with a large snarling dog on the front porch. Mr. Wright said he couldn't remember whether or not the dog would bite so we would just have to find out. He graciously allowed me to get out first and walk toward the house. Fortunately, a lady came to the door and the dog quickly forgot about us. Ms. Culver was the lady who came to the door, and she immediately remembered the conversation she had with my brother at the nursing home. As a matter of fact, she had been expecting me as my brother told her I would be coming by for directions. She went to the back of the house and returned with her mother who had been taking a nap. Between the two of them and Mr. Wright, I learned a lot about early settlers in Cypress Inn and finally got around to asking about directions to the gravesite of John L. Lindsey. Ms. Culver did remember the old cabin and that the small cemetery was on a hilltop surrounded by a lot of pine trees. She remembered having to climb the hill to reach the cemetery when she was a small child. Unfortunately, she was sort of confused about the actual roads and referred us to another lady a few miles down the road who owned the property. Since we would need her permission to scout the area, we drove to her house. There we learned she had sold the property to a dentist, who had an office in Florence. She directed us to a cabin where his son lived and thought we could get permission from him to look around for the grave. Luckily, the son was at home and told us he would ask his father, but he did not think it would be a problem.

The son lived in a cabin as isolated as one could get on this planet. A series of turns onto single lane dirt roads and then onto a long narrow driveway was necessary to reach his house. There must have been a dozen dogs rushing out to greet me but they did not seem menacing. The young man told me his boy could take me to the grave on his four-wheeler if I wanted to go now. Since it was late summer and I was not dressed to confront snakes and ticks, I told him I would return when it was cold enough to discourage those two scourges of the South. In the meantime, he would have time to ask his father about permission. Unfortunately, when cold weather did arrive, I was unable to catch anyone at home. I must have made a dozen trips to the cabin, but no one ever responded to my approach, except the dogs. I was not comfortable walking around the property without permission, so I decided the only solution was for me to visit the dentist at his office in Florence.

Dr. Stoddard, owner of the property, was very gracious and quick to give me permission to search his property for the grave. He was somewhat familiar with the old cemetery on his place and was surprised to learn it was the burial site of a Revolutionary War soldier. Instead of returning to the cabin and dealing with the pack of hounds, I entered the property from another site and looked for a stand of pine trees on a hill. The only problem was that the area was covered with pine trees and was nothing but hills and hollows. My first few trips proved fruitless but I was determined to find the cemetery. My wife was with me on one trip when we encountered two turkey hunters coming out of the woods. They turned out to be the brothers of a fellow who hunted raccoons on our property and did some backhoe work for me. They were hunting on property belonging to their mother, but they grew up in the area and knew exactly where the cemetery was located. Graciously, they offered to take us there and save us the trouble of wandering around in the woods. We walked a considerable way and the last half mile or so found us walking along the top of a ridge. The cemetery was so small and grown up we were in the middle of it before we realized it. I quickly found the grave marker of Sylvester Lindsey, and a depression alongside it was obviously the burial site of the man we had been looking for, John L. Lindsey. The hunters left us as we convinced them we could find our path back to the car. It took a while for it to sink in but the difficult search was finally over. As I looked around, it became evident why I had so much trouble finding the cemetery. It was indeed on the top of a steep hill, but we had accessed the ridge a good way back and did not have to climb the steep hill remembered by Ms. Culver. Also, I found hundreds of huge stumps which were the remains of the pine trees Grace Culver remembered from her childhood. They had obviously been harvested years ago for timber.

During the long search, my brother had arranged for a small marker to be made. Now that the grave site had been located and the marker had been completed, the only task left now was to actually place the marker on the grave. That was easier said than done. It was obviously going to be more than a little bit of trouble to transport a stone weighing over one hundred pounds back into the woods without a passable road anywhere close to the cemetery. I had helped my brother set many gravestones in years past and knew from experience they are extremely heavy and cumbersome. My nephew, Phillip McDonald, came to my rescue when he borrowed a couple of four-wheelers and a small two-wheel trailer from a friend. We were able to load the stone on the trailer, take a field road to the base of the ridge, and then trailblaze a path up to the top of the ridge to the gravesite with the four-wheelers. It would have taken several strong backs all day to do what the four-wheelers accomplished in only a few minutes. We completed this task on a clear, crisp morning and finally, the job was over. It was with a great deal of pride that we took several pictures of the newly erected grave marker and the small cemetery which had been nearly forgotten, except by turkey hunters, for many years. It was an honor to place a marker on the grave of a man who fought for the independence of our great nation. The United States of America became a reality on the backs of such men and they deserve the eternal gratitude of our country. The story of John L. Lindsey can be found in its entirety in my brother's book, *Judi Letters*, in the article entitled, Soldier Boy in Blue.

So, the race against time ended atop a very remote and isolated hill in Wayne County, Tennessee. Knowing from the start that my brother's time on earth was very likely coming to an end pushed me to complete my assignments before he passed away. All that remained was to visit my brother and give him my final report.

Bill and I talked many times about dying, particularly during the last few months of his life. He assured me his "bags were packed and ready to go." In 2006 we lost our brothers, Johnny and Bobby, within two months of each other. In attempting to describe to the simple human mind what heaven will be like, the Bible gives us some amazingly precise measurements and details. Bill talked with all of his brothers about all of us having to face death, but we would agree to meet at the Eastern Gate and there reunite with friends and family who had gone on before us. The Bible plainly states that we will recognize each other when we reach our real home. Undoubtedly, there are those who are aghast at such an arrangement and think it to be nothing but silly superstition. At this point in time, all we can do is simply wait and see.

On my last visit with Bill, I noticed someone had left a CD player and a CD of the Gaither family gospel group. He was too weak to talk, and I suggested we just sit quietly and listen to the Gaither family sing their old-time gospel music. Eye contact told me he agreed with my suggestion so we just sat and listened to the music. It wasn't long before he closed his eyes and seemed to be sleeping, so I took this opportunity to take my leave. On the way to my truck it occurred to me that the song the Gaithers were singing as I left was a song with the title, "Eastern Gate." There is a line in the song which goes, "I will meet you in the morning just inside the Eastern Gate." Bill died early the next morning, and I am convinced beyond a shadow of a doubt there was a joyful reunion at that gate in a place we all call Heaven.

I am reminded of my older brothers almost every day. These memories are triggered by such a host of different occurrences, they would be impossible for me to name. Each of my brothers was as different from the other as night is from day, yet we are alike in so many ways. Each brother taught me things which are both tangible and intangible. From my brother Bill, I learned to milk a cow. He also taught me to always drop three kernels of corn at a time when I planted my garden. One was for the birds, one was for family and one was to give to neighbors. It would probably astonish many folks to learn that my oldest brother could witch for water. There are those who scoff at such a thing but their ignorance is not my problem. As a matter of fact, Bill used a forked apple branch to locate the spot to drill the well at my current home, as well as the house we built when our family moved from East Florence. I saw him do it with my own eyes enough times to believe it is real, and I knew he would never lie to me.

Our parents did not raise any saints, so there were plenty of faults to go around. All of us shared them equally. But, from all my siblings combined, I had at least a glimpse of many of the important intangible things of life: faith, love of family, love of country, honor, generosity, integrity, humor, punctuality, duty, and a responsibility to always keep my word to others. It would be foolish to believe all of them possessed all these traits all the time. Even their little brother knew this was not true, and I have been their biggest fan for a long, long, time. If we are able to go through our life and focus on the good things we find in people and not dwell solely on the not so good, it won't matter at all when we are together again at the Eastern Gate.

******

Also by Tom McDonald

When Memories Come Calling

- Winner of the 2015 USA REBA – Non-Fiction, Southeast

Dirt Road Memories: A Collection of Southern Short Stories

- Winner of the 2016 USA REBA – Non-Fiction, Southeast

Both of Tom McDonald's first publications were selected as southeast regional winners in the non-fiction category for the 2015 and 2016 USA Regional Excellence Book Awards, celebrating works that "truly capture the spirit of the Southeast."

Reviews of McDonald's books have been favorable, particularly for *When Memories Come Calling*. Pat Dye, former Auburn University coach, said, "There ought to be more books written by Tom McDonald."

www.ingramcontent.com/pod-product-compliance
Lightning Source LLC
Chambersburg PA
CBHW021358090426
42742CB00009B/913